WOMEN LIBRARIANS IN INDIA
A Study in Work-Life Balance

Contents

Preface		(*vii*)
List of Tables		(*xi*)
List of Models		(*xv*)
List of Graphs		(*xvii*)
1	Introduction	1
2	Social and Professional Status of Women from past to present	23
3	What it Means to be a Women Professional : View from the Literature	41
4	Research Methodology and Procedure	77
5	Job Satisfaction : A Theoretical Framework	97
6	Demographic profile of Women Library Professionals	120
7	Factors in Job Satisfaction of Women : A Case of Librarians	130
8	Overview and Trends	177
References		196
Index		216

Preface

To present the discussion in lucid way the whole gamut of the present study has been divided in eight chapters including the concluding one. The first chapter is introductory in nature. The brief discussion about the concept of job satisfaction and significance of the job satisfaction has been provided in this chapter. Importance of work in human's life has also been highlighted.

Chapter 2 of the study presented, social and professional status of women from past to present. Here, the social status of women through different periods of civilizations has been discussed. The discussion about the impact of education and women status has also been presented. The role and status of women in the modern era of professionalism has also been discussed. It has been found that the professions in which women have engaged themselves are mainly teaching, medical and health services, nursing and librarianship. These professions seem to be more suitable for women not only because of their professional training but also by their temperament because the women have natural tendency to serve and they are entrusted with work of responsibility and perform their duties very honestly and sincerely.

The entry of women in librarianship has been discussed. Role of Melvil Dewey in women librarianship has also been highlighted in short words. Women's status in librarianship has also been focused.

Chapter 3 presents the review of literature relating to job satisfaction. Review of literature has been divided into 8 parts taken into consideration all the important dimensions of job satisfaction. First chapter is introductory in nature. It has been found that most of studies used primary data to analyze job satisfaction among the employees employed in different libraries. Application of factor analysis and correlation analysis is a common practice among researchers to conclude about the factors affecting job satisfaction. However, a void is still to be filled in the literature. The present study endeavored in the same direction. To analyze the satisfaction among the women library professionals, the advance statistical techniques like Logistic Model, Mann-Whitney non-parametric U-test etc. have been applied to test the factors' significance affecting job satisfaction among the women librarians. The indigenous techniques viz., factor analysis and correlation analysis have also been carried out.

In chapter 4, the research methodology to pursue aforementioned objectives has been discussed. The design of the primary survey to collect the relevant data has been provided along with the statistical techniques applied to test the hypothesis. Sampling technique and pilot survey has also been applied here.

In chapter 5, a theoretical framework of job satisfaction has been designed to present the on-the-job factors and off-the-job factors affecting job satisfaction have been discussed. Job satisfaction of women librarians with the different factors/variables (i.e., on-the-job and off-the-job factors) under different specific dimensions have also been studied. All these factors are affected by each other in some way or the other and correlated to each other either significantly or insignificantly (the empirical proof about the statement has been given in chapter 8).

The chapter 6, deals with the demographic profiles of the respondents i.e., demographical profile of the women librarians from whom the data has been collected.

Chapter 7 is empirical in nature, and discusses the empirical results obtained via applying the different statistical methods viz. Frequency Percentage, Factor Analysis, F-Statistics, Multiple correlation, Step Wise Regression, Ranking, Logistic Regression Model and Mann-whitney non-parametric U-statistics.

The analysis of data collected regarding job satisfaction of women library professionals found no significant difference in the degree of satisfaction caused by on-the-job and off-the-factors. The findings are based on the different dimensions associated to job satisfaction which have been mentioned in chapter 7.

Chapter 8 presented the summary and conclusion of the present study. Findings based on perceptions of women library professional for library profession have also included in the beginning of the same chapter.

List of Tables

5.1 Literature on Job Satisfaction noticed in Library and Information Science Abstracts (LISA)

4.1 Questionnaire Statistics

6.1 Distribution of the sample according to Age

6.2 Distribution of the sample according to Marital Status

6.3 Distribution of the sample according to Husband's Occupational Status

6.4 Distribution of the sample according to Family Background

6.5 Distribution of the sample according to Nature of Family

6.6 Distribution of the sample according to Number of Dependents

6.7 Distribution of the sample according to Academic Qualifications

6.8 Distribution of the sample according to Professional Qualifications

6.9 Distribution of the sample according to Improvement in Qualifications

6.10 Distribution of the sample according to Professional Experience

6.11 Distribution of the sample according to Promotion during Job

6.12 Distribution of the sample according to Designations and Pay Scales

6.13 Distribution of the sample according to Personal Perceptions for other factors affecting Job Satisfaction

7.1 Factors showing Original Motivation for Library Profession

7.2 Factors showing Right Choice of Librarianship

7.3 Ranks given by Academic, Public and Family community for the status of Library Profession

7.4 On-the-job factors showing Satisfaction / Dissatisfaction level

7.5 Off-the-job factors showing Satisfaction/ Dissatisfaction level

7.6 Correlation Matrix of 5×5 showing intercorrelation among the different factors

7.7 Correlation Matrix of 12×12 showing inter correlation among the behavioral components of the supervisor

7.8 Inter Correlation Matrix of 12×12 showing inter correlation among motivational factors for increasing efficiency of work

7.9 Correlation Matrix of 12×12 showing inter correlation among recruitment and promotion policy variates

7.10 Inter-correlation coefficient of job and family relationship variables

7.11 Correlation Matrix of 8×8 showing inter correlation among personal and social factors affecting job satisfaction

7.12 Inter correlation matrix of 8×8 order showing relationship between factors responsible for job dissatisfaction

7.13 Factor analysis applied for the variables concerning Job Satisfaction

7.14 Factors extracted for the variables concerning satisfaction level

7.15 Results pertaining to the Logistic Model applied to obtain the effect of demographic factors on satisfaction

List of Models

1. Motivation Model
2. Job Satisfaction Model
3. Logistic Model

List of GRAPHS

1. Graph showing determinants of Job Satisfaction
2. Bar Chart showing ranks given by respondents to stick to this profession
3. Pie Chart showing ranks given by academic, public and family community for the status of library profession
4. Bar Chart showing priority given by respondents for job Satisfaction
5. Bar Chart showing ranks given by respondents for the most important conditions of Job Satisfaction
6. Bar Chart showing ranks given by respondents for Dissatisfaction with promotion policy

1
Introduction

1.1 CONCEPTUAL BACKGROUND

"Na hi Kascitksanamapi jatu tisthatyakarmakrt Karyate hyavasah karma sarvah prakrti jairgunaih"

Verily, none can even rest for an instant, without performing action, for, all are made to act, helplessly indeed by virtue of prakrti or nature.

(*Yogi, 1967, p.188*)

Ever since, the time of man's arrival on this Good Earth, he must have worked hard for his very survival. We cannot conceive of man even of the primitive times, without doing one kind of work or the other.

Indian culture not only stresses work ethos but suggests that it is necessary for attaining perfection. Work is an important aspect of man's life and behaviour. Man has to devote a good part of his life in the pursuit of his occupation to make a living.

The most active part of man's life is spent in doing some kind of work or work related activities. The relationship between work and man, therefore is of great importance and thus became rich material for poets, writers and philosophers to write, sing, speculate and theorise about work (Rao, 1986, p.1). So, it is natural that work has attracted the attention of poets, psychologists, educationists, philosophers, managers, national planners, behavioral scientists etc. Comprehensive and in-depth studies of the behavioral phenomenon involved in work have been conducted by scientists both in Western as well as in Eastern countries.

Some people like their work while others dislike it. People take a job for their livelihood. Some stay in the same job and organisation for a life time while others are always on the move. Majority of modern men/women have to work in organizations, so they very much effected by the context or environment in which they work. They may like some aspects of their work and its environment. They may have disliking for some aspects of work or they may be indifferent to others. All these attitudes regarding job come under the preview of job satisfaction.

Job satisfaction is satisfaction regarding paid work related dimensions. Job satisfaction is defined as "an attitude which results from a balancing and summation of many specific likes and dislikes experienced in connection with the job (Bullock, 1953, p.9). This attitude maintains itself in evaluation of the job and of the employing organisation. Job satisfaction is rather an evaluation of one's job and employing company as contributing suitably to the attainment of one's personal objectives.

Job satisfaction is governed to a large extent by perceptions and expectations. Men work to satisfy their needs and they aspire or expect their work life to fulfill these needs. For perfect job satisfaction, there should exist one to one relationship between the perception of how well the job fulfills the various needs and expectations or aspirations of the individual and the extent to which these needs are actually fulfilled. Any discrepancy between aspirations and perceptions account for dissatisfaction. The perceived or imagined judgement of how well the job life is satisfying the various social, psychological and economic needs, accounts for the degree of job satisfaction and dissatisfaction.

Men work for various reasons. One individual works he needs money, while another who has million rupees works because he likes power, prestige, social status or the self-respect that is brought about by the job/work. The motives for working change from time to time, differ from one individual to another. It is natural that an individual aims to achieve some goal or objective, which ultimately provides him/her with some sort of satisfaction and if he/she is not able to achieve the aimed objectives, he/she experiences dissatisfaction and frustration.

Most human beings have to do some job where from he/she not only earns his means of livelihood but also aims at deriving some inner satisfaction by showing his/her abilities through job. Greater satisfaction is likely to lead eventually to a more effective functioning of the individual and the organisation as a whole. In fact, working life is to be evaluated not simply in terms of the amount of good turned out, the productive efficiency and the profit it brings, but also in terms of satisfaction which employee derives from it (Lickert, 1961, p.42). Only job satisfaction can lead to quality and efficiency at work place.

Managements are concerned with utilising existing human resources to the optimum level and to make the organistion functional, more efficient and effective. It cannot be translated into reality unless and until managerial people will adopt and adapt policies and practices based on the much needed understanding of worker's perception of job satisfaction, conducive to work adjustment and job involvement. On closer analysis, studies have revealed that job satisfaction is of great significance in the functioning of an organisation (Morse, 1953, p. 18).

Research reveals that the phenomenon of job satisfaction affects not only the organisation efficiency and effectiveness in as much as it avoids dys-functional job behavior and withdrawl behavior, but also like the adjustment and physical health of employees. It serves to reduce behavioural pollutants such as strike, lock out, slow down, work to rule, non-co-operation sabotage etc. in the work environment and improves the quality of life (Garg, 1999, p. 109).

Job satisfaction is a key element which provides an insight into the psychology of work-disability as well as an innovative access to numerous management problems. In order to utilise the existing staff to the best institutional advantage as well as to their own, studies of job satisfaction have often been conducted from time to time in the world of libraries since 1930s, but it is only recently that the significance of such studies has started being felt in the world of libraries (Jones, 1996, p. 270).

Fundamentally, an organisation comes into existence exclusively through the efforts of people. And people working in an organisation are attracted to it because they anticipate that the organisation will offer them rewards that will satisfy their needs.

Expectations from work and its environment vary from person to person, depending upon the values and needs, people perceive. As such, a person experiences different degrees of pleasure or displeasure on different jobs and or with different aspects of the same job. Besides, there are individual differences in the vocational needs of people and in jobs with respect to reinforcers available for the satisfaction of needs.

Research in job satisfaction reveals that the ideal of human efficiency would be the production of maximum output of highest quality in the shortest time with the least expenditure of energy with maximum satisfaction (Poffenberger, 1942, p.78).

Similarly, an organisation can be evaluated in terms of human satisfaction. Thus, it may be concluded that the study of employee's satisfaction in any organisation like a library is an issuc to be given prior consideration to achieve its basic objectives (Morse and Reimer, 1956, p. 123).

Notwithstanding the controversy, a fact that stands out prominently in this century is the earnest desire of all serious thinkers to make work more agreeable, meaningful and interesting to tap the benefits of involvement and motivation at work (Srivastava, 1983, p.74). And the importance of work is still the more in service oriented organisations like libraries because the major scope for their improvement in efficiency and effectiveness comes through a more effective use of human resources (Navalani, 1990, p.86). Sociologists, psychologists, managers and administrators today are preoccupied with designing strategies for providing job satisfaction to all. And job satisfaction has been a favourite research area in India and abroad (Ganguli, 1971, p.226).

Women's role in building the nation is extremely vital. Since the dawn of civilization, women have to carried out very important functions of day to day life. The whole responsibility of carrying out household activities and bringing up the children were all on her shoulders. She was been bound to four walls of the house.

Women, inspite of having brains, had been deprived of superior jobs. The great and powerful woman force comprises of one half of the total population. The vast human resource (i.e women) must be utilized and should not be ignored. It has to be taken care of respected and harnessed effectively for optimum advantage to the women and to the nation for real progress and prosperity.

Realisation of the importance of women force led to the celebration of the International Women Decade (1985-95) and International Women Year since (1994-95). The fact that women have to be studied and understood if the entire society is to be understood and made to progress has been put into force.

Empowering women entreneus is essential for achieving the goals of sustainable development and the bottlenecks hindering their growth must be eradicated to entire full participation in the business. Apart from training programmes, newsletter mentoring, trade fairs and exhibitions can also be a source for entrepreneurial development. As a result, the desired outcomes of the business are quickly achieved and more of remunerative business opportunities are found. Henceforth, promoting entreneurship among women is certainly a short cult to rapid economic growth and development (Panigraphy, 2011).

A remarkable change is currently visible in the occupational arena in India. Women in this country today are seeking education that would equip them for jobs outside their home. As a result, women have reached almost every profession right from flying acroplaner to higher order administration, management and politics. It is a fact that women have dual role, one pertaining to home and other to the job. The dual role creates many problems in that she has multifarious responsibility thrust upon her. In recent years all over the world, women are moving towards equality with men, this equality still increases the burden of women. They have to perform full time household duties and also perform the additional role of a wage earner. Thus, working women have diverse roles which may not always be complementary.

An increasing number of women workers are entering the work arena. Many of them are acquitting themselves well in challenging managerial roles. They continue to face subtle forms of resistance at work place. Some organisations often have the same personal policies, recruitment, selection procedures and promotion criteria for women as for men. They offer extra concessions to their female employees like convenient working hours, transport and creche facilities and easy postings.

A major obstacle for women who aspire to achieve a managerial position is the constraint imposed by society, family and women themselves. Some researchers refer to these constraints as myths, preconceived ideas on unsupported notions. An important factor which hinders a potential female managers in her growth is the paternalistic attitude adopted by the organisation, once again claiming to prove the incapability of women for responsible positions. Many working women have been found to leave their jobs due to sense of pressure being felt probably as a result of their involvement in two demanding areas of office and home.

Despite the fact that the social status of women in India is comparatively lower than in certain developed countries, there are more women managers and administrators in India than in most less developed countries.

In India, on the one hand, one finds complete lack of education among women, denial of separate identity, immobility, lesser role in decision making; on the other hand, one finds women who are leaders in politics, education, administration, different professions and various spheres of life where they take important independent decisions.

Women constitute half of the world's total population but are subjected to inequality and oppression. To effect her complete emancipation and make her equal to man, it is necessary for the national economy to be socialised and for women to participate in common productive labour. Traditionally, men are supposed to be the principal bread winners for the family, while women are left to look after the household chores. Decision making power in the family is regarded as an exclusive male preserve.

It is very distressing but true factor that inspite of all sacrifices, working women are confronted with a number of problems at their work place as well as in their domestic life i.e. conflicts between domestic and official role, transport problems, job environment, unhealthy working conditions, treatment of superiors, attitude of boss, female and male colleagues, promotion policies, over and indirect discrimination from fellow employees, employers, and organisational structure and climate, lack of role models, feeling of isolation, their status at work place and in the family etc., (Swarajyalaxmi, 1992, p.x). All these issues create dissatisfaction.

1.2 OPERATIONAL DEFINITIONS

Historically speaking, the term job satisfaction was brought to lime light by F. Hoppock in 1935 when he published his classic work entitled "Job Satisfaction" (Memoria and Gankar, 2003, p. 647).

In recent years, considerable research has been devoted to study job satisfaction and efforts are going on to have to precise definition. Operational definitions are such as:

The term 'Satisfaction' is derived from the Latin words 'satis' and 'facere' meaning 'enough' and 'to do' respectively. Job satisfaction is an integral component of the organizational climate and an important element in management employees relationship. Job satisfaction may be described in terms of attitude forward the job like any other attitude it represents a complex assemblage of cognition (belief or knowledge), emotions (feelings, sentiment or evaluations) behaviours and tendencies. (Raza and Gupta, 2000, p. 129).

Job Satisfaction

The word 'Job' broadly means a piece of work to be done. It refers to a very specific task. Here it is paid regular employment in an organization.

The expression 'Satisfaction' means the content derived from a piece of work in which the person is engaged. It is essentially related to human needs and their fulfillment through work.

Any combination of psychological, physiological and environmental circumstances that cause a person truthfully to say, "I am satisfied with my job (Hoppock 1935, p.18).

In this definition, the underlying assumption is

that it is possible for a worker to balance satisfaction against specific dissatisfaction and thus arrive at composite satisfaction with the job as a whole. "Job satisfaction has been conceived as the effective orientation of individuals towards work role that they are presently occupying. Satisfaction represents an individual's subjective evaluation and judgements of rewards that he has received" (Vroom, 1964, p. 21).

Khandelwal (2003, p. 246) stated that, job satisfaction has been regarded both as a general attitude as well as satisfaction with specific dimensions of the job such as pay, the work itself, promotion opportunities, supervision, co-workers and so forth. These may interact indifferent ways to create the feeling of satisfaction or otherwise with the job.

1.3 WHAT IS A PROFESSION

A profession is a discipline based practice for welfare and progress of the society. The prominent professions in the ancient world were medicine, law, clergy commerce and military services. Later in the 19th and 20th century, many new professions came up such as science and management. Professions are valued by their services, have their associations. They have degrees in higher/professional education. They have their own body of literature and ethics. Professionals have to continuously update their knowledge and skill. Professions are autonomous in themselves, as their entry/ membership is controlled by themselves.

A profession has been defined in several ways. According to Saunders and Wilson (1937, p. 137) "A profession is defined as the possession of an intellectual technique acquired by special training, which can be applied to some sphere of everyday life."

A profession is considered as performance of certain functions valued in society in general and earning a living as a full time job by these activities.

According to Shaffer (1968, p.81) "A profession specializes in specific knowledge and skills. It endeavours to engage itself in continuous research and updating of specialized knowledge." Profession, infact, is an intellectual activity which fulfills the social necessities of the society. Simply, profession is defined as an occupation having features of monopoly, autonomy and authority.

Professionalism

The character and conduct of people working in a profession is called professionalism.

1.4 LIBRARY PROFESSION

Librarianship was a vocation before Melvil Dewey. In the late 19th century, many events happened to raise this field to the status of a profession. University technical education was started in the late 19th century by opening library schools. Libraries are very old but the science of librarianship emerged slowly in the 19th century. Over the past hundred years or so, librarianship has evolved into a profession both at the national and international levels. It satisfies above said criterion. Librarianship has its associations at local, national and international levels. Its practice requires basic training.

Library management is taught at the university and higher level of education. It has got its own published literature in the form of journals, text books, research reports and electronic publications. Research is constantly being done at the national and international level in universities and higher educational centres. It is enovating its methods and knowledge to cater the needs of the society. It provides services in the form of reference and information sources to satisfy the information needs of different persons in the society. In the information society library and information services are highly valued for the development of individuals and the nation as a whole.

Our profession is growing in strength and has many sub disciplines or specializations.

1.5 LIBRARY PROFESSIONAL

According to Prytherch (2000, p.592) a professional is a member of the professional staff performing work of a nature requiring training and skill in the theoretical or scientific parts of library work as distinct from its merely mechanized parts. A professional is a person who professes in his/her chosen calling. Similarly, a library professional is a professionally trained and formally educated in libraries and information services and serves the community in this area. A library professional may work in an institution or provide services of his/her own, both free and fee based. Providing services is his/her creed.

1.6 WOMEN LIBRARIANS

In the pre-1876 era, library jobs were considered very suitable for the women as people thought that it was an easy and secure job. Librarians were only supposed to arrange books on the shelves and issue them for home reading and keep a record of loan. It was considered clerical and light job. But with the growth and widespread, men dominated the profession when it required lot of research and innovation based service strength of women declined.

But now with the coming of women libraries, this profession has attracted many women at all levels. Now many women librarians are the leaders of the profession, for example, *Ingrid Parent is now the current president of IFLA.* Women have grown in number and their dedication and services to the LIS profession have been recognized. But still women have special problems at the work place. They have responsibility inside and outside the library. Their motivation to contribute in libraries depends upon many factors. Therefore, this study has been undertaken to assess the factors which promote job satisfaction among women librarians in academic librarians of Punjab. It tries to know what affects positively and what affects negatively on the women towards better professional performance.

1.7 STATEMENT OF THE PROBLEM

We have a very rich and ancient cultural heritage which eulogises *"Work As Worship"*. The Holy Gita preaches perfection of work without expectations and return, as also for attainment of *"Moksha"* through *"Karam Yoga"*. Hard work is a part of our cultural heritage. Yet, it is also a fact that work ethics is fast deteriorating in India. Libraries are no exception to it. Top Persons at the helm of libraries complaint about this deteriorating work situation.

Sociologists, psychologists, managers and administrators are paying increasing attention to make work more agreeable, meaningful, stressless and interesting to tap the benefits of motivation and job satisfaction at work. The importance of work and work environment is still more in service oriented organization like Libraries because the major scope of improvement in efficiency and effectiveness comes through a more effective use of human resources i.e.

library professionals; (male + female). Behaviour of professionals in library organization is determined by characteristics of a person interacting with elements in the person's environment. It is a function of the person in environment. Human resources are very important constituents in the organization which convert the financial and material resources into desired services. As the libraries are roots and fruits of the civilization, therefore, unless and until the management utilizes the human resources fully well, libraries cannot accomplish the objective which may aim to achieve it (Navalani, 1990, p. 85). To get out maximum from human resources, the study of job satisfaction and work environment including all on-the-job and off-the-job factors is crucial and needs attention. To manage the library staff effectively, particularly female staff, is very necessary to make them satisfied by providing congential atmosphere.

Libraries are places of work where women play beyond their traditional roles. Women in these libraries have considerable responsibility and they work under formal conditions of complete equality with men. So, in these libraries, greater mutual adjustment by both men and women is necessary to enable women to play their appropriate roles. Reviews of the disabilities and constraints available in literature on position of women in modern society indicate that they are not enjoying the equality guaranteed to them in offices and other work places. There may exist strongly held notions of traditional feminine behaviour. There are several features of work and career within the work situation which could be construed as conspiring against women's chances of success. Where such situation exists, there are social problems; for women cannot work effectively because formal recognition of equality of the sexes has been granted. Their effectiveness as workers may be affected by the male resistence to women both covert and overt. These situations may pose particular problems for women. The difficulties faced by women placed in positions requiring initiative and leadership would be even greater. Men may not be prepared to accept women even as an equal let alone as a superior. At best, they may be prepared to accept a woman as an equal, but they may not relish working under a woman boss or taking orders from her (Devi, 1982, p. 93).

The problems which are faced by the female library professionals in the libraries are going to be revealed by the analysis of available data. Accordingly, this study seeks to enquire into the performance of women in the libraries i.e. how well do they appear to perform their role under the suitable working conditions, working environment, their perceptions towards personnel policies and practices and attitudal aspects i.e. favourable or unfavourable, what is their level of job satisfaction that is available for them to play their role effectively and efficiently. The data analysed how much satisfied they are on the job by showing different factors associated to job satisfaction, the problems and hindrances they face in libraries which restrict them to be satisfied workers.

Keeping in view these problems of women workers, an effort has been made by this study to know what a woman actually wants at work place, how much satisfied a woman worker is. That is why, job satisfaction is the result of individual's perception that is what she expects and what she actually receives. So, this study is primarily meant for examining on-the-job and off-the-job factors create satisfaction and dissatisfaction among the women library professionals working in university and college libraries by accessing their actual position in libraries, their inter personal relations with other employees, the perceptions and attitude of women librarians towards their own position as well as their work, finding out the working conditions, professional growth, attitude, inclination and the treatment that is meted out to women librarians. Their physical and mental steadiness and abilities are also severely affected by the various conflicts, tensions, stresses and strains that are caused for their dissatisfaction on the job are studied.

It is this pathetic situation of the women librarians that has motivated the researcher to take up this problem for the present research work.

1.8 NEED FOR THE STUDY

Job satisfaction of an employee affects the environment of her job, attitude, behaviour and efficiency to fulfil her duties both on job and in family. It is a state of mind inferred indirectly from an employee's response to a question relating to her job. "The human side of enterprise" has become the focal point of modern management. The human side of enterprise is all of a piece that the theoretical assumptions management hold about controlling its human resources determine the whole character of the enterprise. Both the practitioners and theoreticians know the value of meeting human needs in an organisational life and setting. The empirical study of job satisfaction of library professionals and its analysis provides an important diagnostic assessment of the health of organisation i.e. libraries, as also of this segment of library profession in India (McGregor, 1960, p. 32).

Job satisfaction has vital importance for the efficient and effective functioning of every organisation. A literature search has revealed that some studies in job satisfaction were conducted in western countries. These include studies of (Chwe, 1976; D' Elia, 1979; Plate and Stone, 1974; Vaughn, 1972; Vaughn and Dunn, 1974; Wahba, 1975;) etc. and others carried out empirical research on job satisfaction.

All these studies are valuable in understanding the problem of job satisfaction in libraries.

The dearth of published literature on job satisfaction of professional librarians, particularly women librarians in the Indian situation revealed both the lack of interest and difficulty in handling research projects on the part of researchers dealing with female sex as the sample. Most of the works dealing with status and job satisfaction of academic librarians in India are by (Kumar, 1976; Sharma, 1984; Rajagopalan, 1987; Goil, 1978; Sharma, 1972; Gupta, 1972; Verma, 1971; Nandy, 1985). They have dealt with the subject from a general point of view, focussing more or less theoretically the issues leading to their status and job satisfaction whereas only a few combined works female/male have been carried out dealing with one or more specific aspects and dimensions of job satisfaction by (Navalani, 1990; Garg, 1986; Prasad, 1994; Reddy, 1988; Ajit Singh, 1996; Singh, 1995; Khanna, 1981; Chopra, 1984 and Kapoor, 1982).

However, the most recent works carried out by (Parida, 1992 and Samantaray, 1998) leading to Ph.D. degree dealing with the status and job satisfaction of women librarians working in the colleges and universities of Eastern India.

The studies mentioned above are not only regional

in nature but also describe different aspects of job satisfaction.

A careful study of literature reveals that there is no such work done in the colleges and universities of Northern region, particularly dealing with women library professional's job satisfaction. So, the present investigation aims to fill in this gap that exists in the literature on this subject and proposes to focus its thrust taking into account *"Women Librarians in India: a study in work-life balance"*.

1.9 SIGNIFICANCE OF THE PROBLEM

In a developing country like India, professional skills and talent are as scare and important as any other resource. Effective employment of the resources in the most productive way is of utmost importance. The future growth of education and research requires proper organisation and optimum utilisation of resources. The library is one of the principle supporting institutions of higher education and research. It is a dominant agency for conservation/dissemination of knowledge / information. Libraries play constructive role in the fulfillment of our aspirations and programmes of formal education, adult education, family planning, technological development and industrialisation.

For successful functioning of the library and for the performance of manifold duties, libraries require a high degree of technical skills, intelligence, imagination, initiative, efficiency and understanding. As a specialist, a guide, a philosopher, a friend and a social worker, a librarian has to cater to the needs of varied users of the library. She has therefore not only to be professionally qualified, competent and efficient but also to be lively, active, contented and well satisfied with her job. Thus, the need to study the various components of job satisfaction and their effect has become mandatory.

Job satisfaction among librarians both male/ female has been engaging the attention of several researchers by conducting various surveys and studies. It is believed that satisfactory functioning of library and information services depend to a large extent on adequate, appropriate and motivated staffing. This involves:

(i) Attracting staff who are both motivated towards the work and capable of meeting its growing and changing demand

(ii) Employing staff on tasks and under conditions to which they are best suited and in which they can be most effective

Now Research and Development Planning covers the social and human factors which affect worker's motivation and performance of their work place. The effectiveness of every organisation depends on how it transforms inputs into outputs. This process also affects and in returns is also affected by job satisfaction and work committment of employees (Sergean, 1976, p. 30).

From the research findings, it is also evident that the determinants of job satisfaction differ from occupation to occupation and male to female. Hence, it is of the utmost significance to study the job satisfaction of women librarians, who form a different professional group.

The present study of women librarians' job satisfaction would not only throw much wanted light in this barren field, but would also provide an important diagnostic assessment of the health of libraries and climate of women librarian's work life.

1.10 OBJECTIVES OF THE STUDY

1. To measure the level of job satisfaction of women library professionals working in university and college libraries of Punjab.
2. To compare the job satisfaction of women library professionals working in university and college libraries.
3. To study the various factors influencing job satisfaction such as personal factors, factors inherent in job and factors controlled by management.
4. To study the impact of job satisfaction on work culture and professional achievement.
5. To study the main causes of job dissatisfaction among women library professionals.
6. To study the impact of job stress and anxiety on job/work.
7. To study the impact of motivation on job productivity.
8. To find the attitude of employer, supervisor, co-workers, parents and other family members with women workers.
9. To study the status of working women in the family and society.

The findings of this investigation will enable library managers to know the areas of feelings of satisfaction and dissatisfaction among women library professionals, whether seniors or juniors. Information and knowledge about these areas would yield a better understanding of the problems of women professionals and would help the managers in future to get a suitable decision for the proper growth of organisation.

Identification of determinants of satisfaction and dissatisfaction would help in redesigning work for improved quality of working life.

Further, knowledge regarding the differences in job satisfaction among male/female is valuable in understanding them, their needs, their work behaviour and attitudes for the effective results. This information may provide evidence as to which base considerations of modifications and change is the concern of employees, managers and those who concerned with education and training in library and information science.

This survey will help the librarians as well as policy makers to look at the problems of women workers in every field more clearly and closely. Such research will assist library managers in maintaining staff morale and become a basis for effective management.

1.11 HYPOTHESES

Hypotheses are based upon few personal interviews with the women library professionals working in the libraries in different capacities, views of researchers in the field as evidenced from the literature, and some knowledge of the investigator being an employee in university library. The main points which are taken into consideration to formulate hypotheses during the investigation are as follows:

1. Most of the women librarians are dissatisfied due to the stagnation in promotion and poor working conditions.
2. Women's physical and mental steadiness and abilities are also severely affected by the various tensions, conflicts, stresses and strains that are caused for their dissatisfaction on the job.

3. Women librarians with less qualification remain satisfied with what they get from library profession.
4. Social and educational background and job experience of women professionals are related to their satisfaction level on the job.
5. Domestic circumstances do not allow them mobility which affect them to get top positions.
6. Shortage of staff is the reason for increased work load in the libraries which severely affects on their satisfaction level.
7. The attitude of bosses, employers, coworkers and family members are not always congenial for women library professionals to progress and present regularly on their jobs.

2

Social and Professional Status of Women from Past to Present

2.1 INTRODUCTION

"All nations have attained greatness by paying proper respect to the women. That country and that nation which does not respect the women have never become great, nor will ever be in future".

— ***Swami Vivekananda***

In today's world, fermenting with troubles of a variety of national and international issues and fraught with inflation, frustration and unemployment, the very foundations of peace and stability, so vital to human existence are being changed.

In this kaleidoscope, women with their long association with patience and tolerance (particularly in Asia) have a very challenging role to play in effective management of situations, which tend to get out of hand.

In today's society, women's economic emancipation is no longer dependent on men. The time is ripe for women to throw off their shackles of economic dependence and come into their own. It is truly said, "The hand that rocks the cradle, rules the world". It is the women who have sustained the growth of society and moulded the future of nations (Mehta, 2006, p. 1).

In emerging scenario, women have a pivot role to play. It is an accepted fact that women is expected to perform various roles in the society as well as in the family. Women's greater responsibility in the society happens to be the basic unit of a stable society.

The following verse depicts the multifarious duties of an Indian women, especially as the life partner:

कार्येष मंत्री, करणेषु दासी,
भोज्येषु माता, शयतेषु रम्भा।
धर्मे ज्नुकूला क्षमया द्यरित्री,
भार्वा चषाड्गुण्यवतीय दुर्लभा।।

(*Aggrawal, 2005, p.vii*)

Performing duties she gives advice as a minister, in serving she obeys like a maid servant, in feeding she is like mother, as a bed partner she is nymbh Rambha. True companion during religious rites, forbearing like earth; such a life partner possessing these six qualities is very rare.

Serving one's husband and children is neither slavery nor bondage. It is a sacred duty cast upon every women. Kitchen work is also not servitude. A woman, who feels ashamed to cook food for her family, is not a true wife and mother. Her place is not only in the kitchen but it is everywhere. Women and children, being three fourth of India's population, consequently become national human resources (Nisa, 1992, p.40). They are the future of the country. The whole family revolves around the women. Without sacrificing her role as a mother or spiritual head of the family, women has now taken up cudgels of performing multifarious tasks and duties, with the same, in fact will have greater efficiency, dedication and foresight (Rohatagi, 1998, p.12).

Woman of present age possesses managerial skill that has kept this old age institution from crumbling apart against the pressure of society. Women are no longer considered as mere harbingers of peace but are emerging as the source of power and symbol of progress.

Gandhiji had observed that 'Women Power' has abundant potentials. While quoting an article of Gandhiji, published in 1918 in the journal "Young India" stated that:

> "*Women are the companion of men gifted with equal mental capacity. She has the right to participate in the minute details of activities, freedom and liberty*".
>
> — *Kumari & Rao (2005: viii)*

Women can no longer be satisfied by restricting their sphere of activities to three K's, viz., Kitchen, Kids and Knitting.

Similarly, Pt. Jawahar Lal Nehru (1889-1964) rightly observes that

> "*To awaken the people, it is the women who must be awakened. Once she is on the move, the family moves, the village moves and the nation moves*".
>
> — (*Aggarwal, 2005, p. viii*).

2.2 SOCIAL STATUS OF WOMAN THROUGH DIFFERENT PERIODS OF CIVILIZATION

The worth of a civilization can be judged from the position that it gives to women. Of the several factors that justify the greatness of India's ancient culture, one of the greatest is the honoured place ascribed to women. Manu, the great law-giver, said long ago, "Where women are honoured there reside the Gods". According to ancient Hindu scriptures, no religious rites can be performed with perfection by a man without the participation of his wife. Wives are thus befittingly called "ARDHANGANI" (better half). They are given not only important but equal position with men (Kaur, 2005, p.156).

The position of women in society indicates their cultural, spiritual and social attainments. Treatises have been written on the status and position of women through different ages. Status is directly related to role and where role is important, status would naturally be good and satisfactory. This truth applies to women also. Through history, the role of women has been alloted and viewed differently by different historians, social scientists and women's studies by experts in different periods, under the influence of existing conditions. It is an accepted fact that women had good status more or less equal to that of man in ancient India.

During the early Vedic period, it is generally believed that women enjoyed relatively high and respectable position in Indian society, but during the later vedic period, the status of women degraded and lots of restrictions came to be imposed on them.

The Hindu woman improved her social status during the post independence period. Her legal disabilities with regard to marriage, inheritance, guardianship and adoption have been removed. She inherits the property of her father.

In Rig Vedic age (2500 BC – 1500 BC), the position of women was quite satisfactory. Right of education was given to girls.

Age of later Samhitas, Brahmans and Upanishads (1500 BC-500 BC), women continued to have a satisfactory status. Education was there for girls and they had the right to say in selection of their life partners.

Epic age was quite glorious age for women.

Age of Shastras and early Samritis (500 BC – 500 AD), was called dark age for women. This was the period when gradual deterioration in position of women began (Rehman, 2005, p. 47-48).

During the period of Mughal Rule, the position of women slumped furthur. It touched the lowest ebb.

During the British Period, women occupied a subjugated and inferior position in society and they seem like "Dumb Driven Cattle" (Swarajalaxmi, 1992, p. 2).

2.3 WOMEN DURING PRE-INDEPENDENCE PERIOD

In the 19th and early 20th centuries, there was an improvement in the status of women. Various factors were responsible for it. Two major movements that affected women's position during the period were the Social Reforms Movement of 19th century and The Nationalist Movement of 20th century. Spread of education was an important factor to bring social change and to improve women's status. Education, Nationalist movement under Mahatama Gandhi's leadership and setting up of Bramho Samaj by Raja Rammohan Roy are considered important to uplift women in this period. Both movements raised the efforts for equal status of women with men. In response to the call of Gandhi named 'Equality', women discarded their veil and came out of the four walls of their houses to fight the battle of freedom. The result is that indian constitution today has given to women equal status with men. There is no discrimination between men and women. All professions are open to both of them with merit, as the only criterion of selection.

2.4 WOMEN AFTER INDEPENDENCE

In modern India, many legislative and social measures were taken to improve the condition of women who had to face cruelty and exploitation in their social life. With the advent of women's education on which the reformers of renaissance laid much emphasis and also with the influence of the West, women revolted against the restrictive norms of traditions. Consequently, the society was compelled to give them equal right to participate in every field of life. After independence, several legislations were enacted to improve the status of women. Spread of education has created a sentiment of self regard into them and women have come forward to claim equal rights. Concern for improving women's status became a national issue when the "National Committee on the status of women in India 1971-1974" published a report of its investigation in 1975 which was entitled "Towards Equality".

2.5 EDUCATION AND WOMEN

Gandhiji had stated long back to evaluate the importance of education for women that "Educating a man is educating an individual while Educating a women is educating a family" (Rehman, 2005, p.53).

Education of women created a certain measure of independence of thought, a spirit of inquiry and objectivity among them. Higher education among them has also created a tendency in them to seek economic freedom. Women are now competing in almost every field with male counterparts (Chand, 2003, p.209).

Education has worked as the prime factor to motivate the women to work. It has opened up more employment opportunities for women to be employed in various professions. They feel that whatever they have acquired through education has to be utilised and not wasted. They should make proper use of their abilities and do something for the service of society, nation, family and for the humanity as a whole. Due to various social, economic and political legal reasons, women started to take up jobs or occupations which were considerable by the society to be respectable for them. They want to use their leisure time in some gainful activity. They are fully conscious of their own individuality and want to maintain their personal status and independent social standing by working and earnings for their own needs. They want to be self-sufficient and understand very well that economic self-sufficiency improves their family standard and their own status.

In short, education and self earnings have increased their self-confidence and now they are able to come out of dependency.

This is the outstanding achievement of modern age in women's context. "The changing status of working women in India" also stated that women have begun to realise that job can raise women's self-esteem, self-confidence and can accomplish their social psychological security and freedom (Kapoor, 1974, p.46)..

2.6 PROFESSIONAL STATUS OF WORKING WOMEN

On viewing from global angle, it appears

appropriate that 20th century is an epoch-making century in the history of humanity which witnessed tremendous changes in every fabric of human life. The phenomenal growth of science and technology, advancement of new knowledge and effectively organised social reform movements have significantly contributed in revolutionising the thinking of men in every path of life and loosened most of the shackles of customs and traditions. On account of these changes, a new complexion of socio-political economic environment has emerged over the whole world. Consequently, socio-economic attitudes and approaches towards "WOMEN" have undergone a vital change. It has been evidently projected in the trends of ever increasing number of women in gainful employment (Mathur, 2000, p.1).

The development of education among women has affected their employment. The increased opportunities for professional training and education have enhanced their employment potential (Swarajyalaxmi, 1992, p.15). Greater geographical and occupational mobility and the emergence of new economic patterns are the main factors of their employment trend (Reddy, 1986, p.14).

With the dawn of independence in our country, women have been progressively absorbed into the mainstream of economic life and they are in fact today in the forefront in many areas of economic and social activities. Women play a crucial role in the economic welfare of the family. It is worth maintaining the inter-relationship of the male and female roles here. Men and women are actors in a complex social and ecological system, which functions reasonably smoothly and provides benefits to both the sexes (Reddy, 1985, p. 4). Regarding the working pattern of the women, it largely depends on two factors; namely (i) need for augmenting the family income and (ii) opportunities for participating in nation building and economic activities. With employment, women don't remain objects of social change, but become its agents.

In one of the International Labour Organisation (1991) studies dealing with women's employment, it was presumed that, motives differed with marital status, both, objectively and subjectively. Not only the economic needs but also the motivational reasons vary with marital status. There are two reasons for women's employment: (a) women's economic needs and (b) national necessity for increased production (Talwar, 1984, p.38-39).

Some other studies have brought to light the fact that loneliness is a powerful motive for women to seek employment. Women's desire for economic independence is for securing higher standard of living. Educated women take up some gainful employment, not necessarily, out of mere economic stringency but also for the sake of making use of their acquired abilities as well as usefully employing their leisure time (Gupta,1983, p. 22).

A study of middle class women, who have sought employment, reveals that the most significant and obvious reasons for taking of employment are to supplement income and fruitfully utilise their education. Ministry of Labour, Government of India (1988) pointed out that four factors prevail, which lead women to join the working force. They are (a) Supplementing the income (b) mishap, such as incapability of the bread winner (c) death of the bread winner (d) women's desire for economic independence or for securing higher standard of living. It reveals that educated women work partly to acquire economic independence and partly to escape from domestic life. They also work for self-fulfillment, because the expectations of women are different from those of men. Their needs and sometimes their level of aspirations are also different from men (Samantaray, 1998, p. 5-6). It was found that, due to dual responsibility, women take up teaching and nursing jobs in large number. The traditional concept of women bondaged to the household, of child rearing and domestic miscellany is now, gradually being changed. Despite the changes, women's position has not totally improved. Male domination still persists. After her return from work, she has to continue the domestic chores (Kumar, 1992, p.198).

From a situation where women have been confined to the role of housewife and mother or in traditional occupations but as a result of their newly gained freedom, women have distinguished themselves in various spheres of life as politicians, orators, lawyers, doctors, administrators, diplomats, teachers, librarians, nurses and social workers etc. Now they are also going army and police, and air pilots.

Among these, the professions in which women have engaged themselves are mainly teaching, medical and health services, nursing and librarianship. These professions seem to be more suitable for women not only because of their professional training but also by their temperament because the women have natural tendency to serve, and they are entrusted with work of responsibility and perform their duties very honestly and sincerely.

2.7 LIBRARIANSHIP AS A PROFESSION FOR WOMEN

The twentieth century has witnessed a sea of

change in the women's liberation from traditional life style and work ethos. The social stereotype is clearly reflected in the divisions of professions which need specific training and higher education. Academic, scientific professions, research and law, etc. are male oriented and male dominated professions. To begin with the middle class, Indian women started taking jobs as opportunities opened to them because of industrialization process. But their entrance into the workforce was likely to teaching, social work and medical professions. Next to teaching, librarianship is considered as a women-intensive profession. These professions are service professions seemed to suit the stereo type of Indian women. Later on equal constitutional rights to both sexes conferred and women's movement for equal opportunities in every field deepened. All these efforts made, succeeded in bringing more women into forefront and enabled them to participate in public life and holding decision-making positions, which were once perceived as male domain (Pradhan, 2006, p. 63).

The history of women in librarianship profession dates back to 1940s in India. In 1942, Bangal Legislation Assembly employed the first qualified woman librarian credited with occupying a key post in India named Anadibai Prabhudesai who was a superintendent of Children's Library in Baroda (Kumar, 1975, p. 222). Thereafter, it was only during the last three decade that more number of women entered into this profession. In the developed countries where librarianship became a female dominated profession because women were regarded as cheap labour force. In India, it is the stereotype of Indian women mainly responsible for making the occupation women intensive librarianship which commands a low status in the society till now, soon found women to be suitable for that job in a man's world. The librarian's job is perceived as routine, trouble-free, non-challenging, time consuming, labour intensive and requires less intelligence, women got accommodated in this profession (Pradhan, 2006, p. 64). But if we dwell into why women select librarianship as a career, there are five main reasons (a) It is a noble profession for women who are interested in learning as well as meeting and serving the learned ; (b) Women perceive this job as a genteel occupation which suits their intelligence and emotional needs; (c) For librarians' job it is not necessary to be mobile which otherwise proves to be a hindrance for the women to stay away from family; (d) Library environment provides a safe and secure workplace and for women security is regarded as the most essential criteria before taking a job; and (e) The library activities are not so hard pressing so that they can do justice to the double burden and workplace and home. Apart from these, there are other factors like (i) nature has bestowed women with qualities of patience, sympathy and perseverance, which are also the vital requisites for successful librarianship. So, it is a good alternative to teaching for the women to pursue; it is a socially acceptable career for women, qualities expected from the librarian suit women; library jobs can be done by women in seclusion without the involvement of male colleagues and away from public (Dasgupta, 1998, p. 245).

Now, more than half of the library and information workforce is constituted of women. They are working in various type of libraries and also in national and regional information centres throughout India and it is more true in western countries. In the United States 82 percent of citizens reporting their occupation in the libraries are women. While they constitute majority of practitioners in librarianship, they are vastly under represented in management roles. The top positions in large libraries usually go to males while it is not so in public and school libraries. More library educators are males than females and more males than females have earned Ph.D. in librarianship. The major commercial professional journals are edited by men though most of the staff members working on them are women (Kaula, 2004, p. 299).

2.8 WOMEN DOMINATED PROFESSION

The (British) Library Association (LA) made an investigation on "Women in Librarianship" in 1966 in which it was observed: "There is concern today regarding the social wastage of women, particularly those who are graduates and those who hold professional qualifications. It appeared that a systematic investigation of "Women in Librarianship" was justified and that the following points needed investigation (1) The shortage of staff in libraries. (2) Whether there was a "reservoir" of qualified married women wishing to re-enter librarianship. (3) Whether there were any steps that could be taken to assist and encourage their return to librarianship.

United States has gone a little further. In an article published in the *Library journal* in 1970, it observed "it is ironic that the profession which was 90 percent female in 1940 and is still numerically dominated by women, may prove especially difficult to rule that is harder for a woman to be appointed or promoted to a leadership position that it is for a man; this happens because men occupy the posts and receive the greatest remuneration." It was observed that, educated women, while meeting resistance in other more established professions, flooded into library work during the last quarter of the 19th century for a variety of reasons (Garrison, 1979, p.56). Librarianship was a new and fast growing field in need of low paid but educated recruits. With the plentiful library jobs available, male librarians offered no position to the proliferation of women library workers partly because women agreed that their library work matched presumed feminine limitations. Melvil Dewey, the father of modern librarianship, had faith in the aptitude of women to library work and service. He could predict when writing at the turn of the century to the ideal librarian that "most of the librarians who achieved this greatness will be women". But the most honoured and well paid librarians were men. The "best" librarians were indeed not made, but born-and born male, was the general observation.

Librarianship in the West continues to include enough women to make it a women's profession. It will remain women's profession by 2000 A.D. and after that, but men may vary well predominate in certain types of libraries, particularly academic, where their percentage has gone beyond 44 percent of professionals. Special and public libraries will also reflect a change in the male-female ratio, with special libraries swinging towards balanced employment of men and women. At the same time, women have been pushing for admittance to higher positions based on their merit. A gender breakdown of various aspects of librarianship other than administration, is not readily available. Since the profession is 84 percent females and more males than females hold the bulk. Of administrative positions, one might conclude that the technical support, readers services and computer operations are composed of women. But there is a general impression that men may be more populous in the automation and information science (Rajyalaxmi, 1999, p.311)

2.9 MELVIL DEWEY AS APOSTLE OF WOMEN LIBRARIANSHIP

It was Melvil Dewey (1851-1931) who for the first time visualized the need and role of more and more women in the field of librarianship. He encouraged women to enter the profession, due to his good faith and confidence in women's ability to discharge the duties of librarianship more efficiently and effectively. When he started first Library School in 1887 with this intention only, he admitted seventeen ladies to the school against the rules of Columbia University in the U.S. He was asked to explain his conduct as the college was not a co-education institution. He had to leave his job but later admitted the girls again at the Library School at Albany against the rules. He was asked to explain his conduct and finally his services were terminated. A pioneer indeed, Melvil Dewey lost his job on the plea that women should be admitted to librarianship. For the first time in the history of training in librarianship in India, four Bengali girls were admitted in the summer course of training conducted by Bengali Library Association (BLA) in 1940 (Kumar, 1975, p. 222).

2.10 WOMEN'S STATUS IN LIBRARIANSHIP

The "Status" refers to one's position in relation to others. Social status in a society is important for human beings. It brigs recognition, power and influence over others. Economic status is very much linked with it. In Maslow's pyramid of human needs, next to security what one wants is social recognition and status. Social status of a professional class being intangible in nature and is accorded by the society. It is value index of services of a particular profession to the society at large. Status is something which is neither given on a plate nor it can be demanded or achieved by force or by all talks or by fat salaries. Status is defined as "the rank or position of an individual in the prestige hierarchy of a group of community (Satija, 2003, p.5).

Every individual has a status position within each group of which he or she is a member and every group has status position within the larger social system (Halloran, 1978, p. 399). Theoretically, status has been defined as the reward and prestige that person can expect who performs a particular role, such as the ranking of social position in terms of power, prestige and esteem in comparison with another or other social positions or as a place in a graded order of power, rank and esteem (Verma, 1992, p. 91). Thus, the status of a person and the role he or she plays in a particular context are usually linked. Therefore, women's status could be the ranking in terms of prestige, power or esteem.

The urge to professionalise occupational groups can be attributed to the status of individuals comprising the "Profession". Librarianship as a profession has its own status in the society. The factors concerning the status involve identity and professionalism which are related to the librarian's educational background, their activity in the profession and the manner in which they view themselves in the academic world (Samantaray, 1998, p.7).

In India, librarianship has been recognized and given professional status. New status for library professionals lies in changing the traditional image of this profession. But it is observed from the surveys that women's status in the library profession is not given as compared to that in other professions.

University Grants Commission (UGC) has also brought the librarians at par with teachers. Status and pay hierarchy of librarians in academic institutes should correspond to the academic staff, in public libraries to those in the educational cadre and in other libraries to those of technical personnel. This practice is prevalent in India. Research shows that the librarians of USA and Grant Britain are satisfied with getting faculty status (Sharma, 1977, p.170). It is found that librarians male/female in Canada have achieved their goal. Upward by mobile librarians enjoy higher salary than immobile librarians. Men tend to move more than women (Harris and Tague, 1989, p. 117). It is observed by (Clow, 1986, p.116) that in France, the library part is characterized by heavy centralization of both career and professional education, whereas Soviet librarians enjoy a respected position.

Library Association Annual Report (1978) reveals that about 60 percent professional librarians working in English public libraries were females.

Library Association Annual Report (1980) reveals that 20.8 percent were men and 79.1 percent were women. Majority of American librarians were women yet women were appointed to fewer than half of the senior posts (Heim, 1987, p. 43).

In general, about 70 percent librarians were women but not many hold leading posts in large libraries (Gundel, 1989, p.447). Annual survey data from 1976-77 to 1983-84 reveals that majority of women as university librarians are still clustered at lower levels of status and pay (Rayman and Goudy, 1980, p. 46).

Usually, it is observed that women's status in the

profession is low. The female image of the profession as librarians is an important reason for the lower status (Prins, 1991, p.18). The following reasons (coined by Ritchie, 1982, p.24) may be relevant (i) Women have less ambition in comparison to men, (ii) Women do not stick to the profession, (iii) Women are less committed to the profession than to the family (iv) Women have less managerial capabilities.

Administration clearly remains a male bastion. However, the women administrators, who have achieved extraordinary success have some common characteristics like a strong sense of femaleness, patience, mobility, openness, determination and professional aggressiveness. Women tend to work harder in libraries just to prove themselves skilled ones.

Even then, few women reach the top jobs in librarianship. It is found in South Africa that in spite of the predominance of women in the profession, 44 to 61 positions are held by men (Louw, 1989, p. 307).

But now, the time has been changed and the entry of females in librarianship has been grown fast. Today's female has been made aware to gain her prestige and status, self esteem and respect in the libraries. She is making fast efforts continuously to arise and to get top positions in librarianship as well as another administrative fields. They are getting higher education and remain always in touch with information technology to cope with the rising demands of computerization in librarianship. Literature on the status of female in libraries indicates towards this fact.

3

What it Means to be A Women Professional : View from the Literature

INTRODUCTION

Primitive man's conceptualisation of work is reflected in a very prepotent survival need. During man's development, the immediate need for work could be defined in terms of activities being oriented towards the acquisition of food and shelter. In essence, there was little differentiation conceptually between the dimensions of life and the dimensions of work.

With the advancement of society and culture, industrialization and material growth, the situation changed. Nevertheless, work remains an important facet of man's life. Man works for earning his livelihood. A man's working life spans forty to fifty years. A survey of Morse and Weiss (1955, P.26) indicates that people like to work even if they inherited enough money to live comfortably. According to Schumacher (1980, P.3), "A person's work is undoubtedly one of the most decisive formative influences on the character and personality". "At the heart of the system of our work lies in our system of values and more precisely, our view of the individual and his relationship with others".

The intricacies involved in work have attracted interests and energies of poets, philosophers, psychologists, managers, researchers and academicians.

The importance of work reflected by the poet Kahlil Gibran 1883-1931, in the words that work in love made visible.

"And if you cannot work with love but only with distaste, it is better that you should leave your work and sit at the gate of the temple and take alms of those who work with joy" (Gibran, 1966, P.35).

Modern men/women work in organisations. The twin objectives which are universally held valid for an organisation, are productivity and satisfaction – productivity for the organisation and satisfaction for its employees. (Sinha, 1981, P.440)

Work provides the major source of satisfaction in adult life. The strongest predictor of longevity, it is claimed, is work satisfaction and absence of job satisfaction is related to heart disease and a variety of mental problems.

The pioneer in the field of employee attitude was Houser (1927). But the first classic work on job satisfaction is by Hoppock (1935). Ever since then "literary thousands of job satisfaction and employee attitude surveys have been conducted and hundreds of articles written on the topic (Dawis et al., 1974, P.55)."

The importance of any topic can be judged by a number of studies, theories and models which have been propounded to explain the particular topic in detail and interesting way. A review of published literature from 1960 to date reflects on the different aspects/dimensions related to job satisfaction in different professional fields published by various scholars and subject experts e.g. job satisfaction among teachers, doctors, bank employees, management, nurses, lawyers and factory workers etc.

In simple words, 'review' means retrospection, to survey, to look back on, or to view it again. Tefko (1981, P.155) defines 'a review' as, a critical synthesis of the state of knowledge in a given subject of topics; it is a critical examination of information and literature on a subject or topic accommodated in its broader framework.

It means it is not a casual reading like reading of story or novel. It focuses and is directed towards a specific purpose. It is also selective. A researcher has to select the kinds of literature to be reviewed and determine the purpose for which she/he has to study them. Because no one is fully conversant with what has gone before, has little chance of making a worthwhile contribution. Therefore, a researcher has to survey the available literature relating to his/her field of study.

In Library Science field, many attempts have also been made to know job satisfaction among library professionals including males/females working in different libraries in India and abroad from time to time by the subject experts and researchers. So, an attempts has been made here to explore theoretical literature and research studies already done on job satisfaction and its related concepts to form the foundations upon which this research work is built

THE PURPOSE OF REVIEW

1. To give a background knowledge of the research topic
2. To identity the concepts relating to it, potential relationship between them and formulated researchable objectives
3. To identify appropriate methodology, research design, methods of measuring concepts and techniques of analysis.
4. To identify data sources used by other researcher
5. To learn about the structure of the reports of others

The Published works on job satisfaction in India and abroad are divided under the following headings i.e. job satisfaction deals with general aspects, women librarians, motivation, job stress, demographics, participative management and information technology.

3.1 JOB SATISFACTION IN GENERAL

Vaughan (1972) carried out the first full scale investigation of job satisfaction of librarians. His hypothesis was that organizational effectiveness in an organization was likely closely to the concept of "job satisfaction" and "employee's satisfactions" and these two concepts are closely related to managerial behaviour. The instrument for collecting data was "Job Descriptive Index (JDI)" designed by Smith, Kendall and Hulin (1969). His sample comprised 107 full time library professionals. The analysis of data was done with the help of computerizing correlation, multivariate and regression analysis as statistical techniques. He measured relationships existing between six dimensions of job satisfaction and forty eight biographical and organizational variables. His findings were that overall satisfaction was linked directly to age, earnings, job level and library science major; and satisfaction with work was directly related to tenure, earning, job level, supervisor's status etc. But his study was limited to one university library.

Vaughan and Dunn (1974) studied job satisfaction among the library employees of six university libraries. They compared the five dimensions; supervision, work, pay, promotion and interpersonal relations. They also compared job satisfaction of various departments in university libraries. They reported that in general, no one department scored consistently high or low in all dimensions in their study.

Wood (1975) studied job satisfaction of students of Sheffield School of Librarianship and Information Studies. A questionnaire was sent to all the students of the School who completed courses from 1965-1973. Ninety five questionnaires were returned. She found that majority of respondents were satisfied with the posts held, freedom to develop one's own ideas, to develop one's professional skills and subject knowledge. The most dissatisfying factors were lack of supporting facilities as staff, equipment, pressure of work, organization of works, working conditions and nature of work.

Chwe (1976) designed his investigation to determine whether librarians were more satisfied with their job than cataloguers in university library environment. 185 reference librarians and 170 cataloguers from 94 university libraries of various sizes in USA responded to his Minnesota Satisfaction Questionnaire (MSQ) administered for collection of data. The findings showed no significant difference in the level of overall job satisfaction between the two groups. However, cataloguers were significantly less satisfied than reference librarians, with three industrial aspects of their job : creativity, social science and variety. He also examined the intrinsic and extrinsic dimensions of job satisfaction. His findings seem to provide some evidence to support although not completely, the motivation-hygiene theory Fredrick Herzberg.

Simmons (1980) conducted a survey in libraries of North London to determine the levels of job satisfaction and styles of supervision among librarians in the libraries. The Centre for Library and Information Management (CLAM) carried out a survey on different aspects of job satisfaction in some U.K. libraries. The investigation elicited opinions from library staff towards their job, comparing and contrasting their perceptions of job enhancement factors. 151 questionnaires were completed. Evidence from the survey indicated that unlike other working groups, the greatest conflict in libraries was not between managers and employees but between professional and non-professionals.

Stead and Scamell (1981) discussed the concept of assertiveness training which had been found to have a positive impact on personal satisfaction. They examined the relationship between assertiveness and individual dimensions of job satisfaction for a sample of 68 professional librarians. Job satisfaction was measured by the Job Descriptive Index (JDI) developed by Smith, Kendall and Hulin. Their findings do not support the current emphasis on assertiveness training, if overall job satisfaction is the goal. Assertiveness training, if overall job satisfaction is the goal. Assertiveness training for the low assertive people may increase their satisfaction with work. Otherwise, it appeared that assertiveness training has little relationship to any other dimension of job satisfaction. In fact, the results suggested that assertiveness training may lead to decrease in satisfaction with co-workers for older, more experienced employees and decrease in satisfaction with supervision for less experienced employees.

Burgess (1982) investigated job satisfaction of Australian University librarians and used the Minnesota Satisfaction Questionnaire (MSQ) for the purpose. The study was carried out by means of questionnaires sent to the total population of 229 librarians. But ultimately the sample comprised of 96 librarians of which 64 were cataloguers and 32 were reference librarians. She reported no difference in the level of job satisfaction between reference librarians and cataloguers as reported in other studies by Chwe. She also found that the cataloguers were less satisfied with the social service aspect of their job. The three least satisfying dimensions were the same for both groups, i.e. advancement, library policies and practices and recognition. And for cataloguers only, the higher position, the greater the career length and age, the higher the level of job satisfaction.

Bhushan Lal (1984) reported an important study on factors related to employees performance. The study has been based on the preposition that a happy worker is a productive worker and satisfaction causes productivity. The study aimed at exploring the relationship between structural, functional and personal factors, that are associated with employee's performance. The sample for the investigation was drawn from three types of library organizations, namely (a) academic university library (b) special and (c) public libraries. The number of respondents from above three categories of libraries under study was 318. In all, several instruments for the measurement of variables have been used. The variables included in the study were (i) Demographic (ii) Psychological-motivation, locus of control, job satisfaction, job involvement, work involvement, job performance iii) Situational-organisational climate. The findings of the study indicate dominance of the male subjects with respect to their level of job performance.

Russell (1984) conducted a study of 341 part time and full time professional library staff in six British academic and public libraries by using MSQ, providing 20 dimensions with various aspects of job. The study revealed that 85% professionals were satisfied with their job characteristics. The causes of the dissatisfaction of library professionals were the nature of the supervision received and lack of freedom of action in the performance of their duties. The most unsatisfactory aspects of their jobs were library policies particularly their promotion and career prospects, their treatment by library management and relationship with professional staff. Success of satisfaction centered on their actual duties and their coworkers.

Nkereuman (1986) studied the issues of correlation between job performance, job attitude and work behaviour among the staff in academic libraries of Nigeria. He pointed out positive but casual correlation between job satisfaction and productivity. Internal and external factors including attitude towards job, daily predisposition also determine the job satisfaction.

Bundy (1988) compared job satisfaction of subject and reference librarians to cataloguers in British and Australian Poltechnics. 163 librarians were surveyed by using MSQ and found higher job satisfaction in subject librarians than the cataloguers and reference librarians. He found that activity was the most satisfying dimension for subject librarians and the factors that create the most dissatisfaction are those which are controlled by institutional and library management such as security, recognition and authority.

Nandy (1988) studied job satisfaction of library professionals and found some methods by surveying several studies in library field. He highlighted the methods to increase job satisfaction and concluded that job satisfaction leads to the effective functioning of an organization as a whole and characteristics of both the individual as well as of the job appeared to be related to job satisfaction but they were inter correlated to such an extent that it was extremely difficult to isolate them for scientific investigation. He concluded that satisfied worker will be a productive worker.

Nkereuman (1990) reported the study carried on to examine the satisfaction and job attitude between professional and non-professionals in the area of promotion and job development. Issues on relationship between job attitude and work behaviour among the staff in academic libraries of Nigeria were chosen to investigate. He brought out that positive correlation between job satisfaction, performance and work behaviour was helpful for better output. He pleaded that job satisfaction might increase with better earnings (good salary) and other rewarding situations like praise and higher studies.

Goulding (1991) stated that non-professional library staff are vital members of staff whose job work can be routine but indispensable. Keeping such staff within the organization is becoming difficult; keeping them and maintaining their job satisfaction is even more of a challenge. Surveys the literature to provide some guidance through this management issue.

Abifarin (1992) discusses results of a study conducted to identify the attributes that are desirable and essential for successfully performing line duties in Nigerian university libraries. The study used the point plan of Professor Alex Rodger of the National Institute of Industrial Psychology, London, UK, and was administrated in questionnaire form to university librarians in the 30 federal and state universities in Nigeria. Discuss the job specification for these libraries which was based on results of the investigation.

Siggins (1992) remarks that research libraries are challenged with retaining an effective staff who have skills to respond to changing circumstances and increased demands. Ways must be found to reduce stress and prevent burnout and also to sustain a level of interest and job satisfaction among staff to ensure a high level of performance. Analyses the elements of job attitudes and their relationship to perform output. Explores factors which lead to job satisfaction and dissatisfaction. Recommends ways in which library administrators and managers can improve job satisfaction.

Oladokun (1993) surveys the status and job satisfaction of paraprofessional library staff in Nigerian libraries. Highlights a degree of satisfaction and considers areas of particular discontent. Discusses the reasons for their choice of the career in librarianship and their mobility and progress within the profession.

Palmer and East (1993) conducted a survey of support staff in twelve state supported academic libraries in Ohio. Satisfaction was reported in five job dimensions (Supervision, Coworkers, work, benefits and pay) but workers were dissatisfied in four dimensions operational procedures, communication rewards and promotion). Results revealed that there was dissatisfaction among technical workers. Satisfaction was high among part-time workers except for promotion, higher for women than for men.

Demers (1994) reported the study, drawing on social system and reference group theory, this study hypothesized that top editors at large newspapers would be more satisfied with their jobs than top editors at small newspapers. Editors on larger newspapers were expected to be more satisfied because increased role specialization gives them greater autonomy, their salaries are higher, and their jobs are more prestigious. A national probability sample of the editors at daily newspapers in the USA supports the hypotheses that editors at larger newspapers are more satisfied and that autonomy is a mediating factor, but income is not related to job satisfaction.

Doyle (1994) presented a survey on the job satisfaction levels of US and international college and university media specialists based on the (Minnesota Satisfaction Questionnaire (MSQ). The MSQ contains 100 questions designed to measure an employee's level of job satisfaction. Discusses job satisfaction theories including Human Relations, work itself, and Physical-Economic Relations.

Voelck (1994) distributed a job satisfaction questionnaire to library professionals in 13 state supported academic libraries in Michigan. This study is a partial replication of a study conducted by Palmer and East (1989). Results indicate that while support staff are satisfied with supervision, nature of their work, co-workers and benefits, they are dissatisfied with opportunities for promotion, pay and contingent rewards. The means of several dimensions of job satisfaction varied significantly by the staff variables of experience, education, position, title, union representation, full or part time work and working directly with users. These results differ in some respects from those reported by Palmer and East. Suggests some ways to improve library professional staff's job satisfaction based on the results of this study.

Hovekamp (1995) reported that previous research pertaining mostly to blue collar uninized workers indicated that the reported job satisfaction among these employees tends to be lower than among non unionized workers. Reports on a study which re-examined this issue through a survey of professional librarians in 19 nonunion and 13 union academic research institutions in the USA. By comparing the survey results of union and non-union participants, the study found that the presence of union has a negative relationship with job satisfaction. However, the results did not support the argument that such a relationship is a product of union culture, as some researchers have suggested. Salary was revealed as a more consistent predictor of job satisfaction. There was also the suggestions that part-time employment status might relate to the survey participants' happiness with their job.

Koenig and Morrison (1996) reports result of a questionnaire survey of library directors of all Association of Research Libraries (ARL) to investigate the relationship between job turnover and job satisfaction of ARL university library directors relative to faculty status. Results indicated a positive relationship between job satisfaction and faculty status. The provision of staff release time to pursue scholarly endeavours was correlated positively with directors reported job satisfaction, whereas hollow faculty status defined as nominal faculty status but without the provision of release time, was correlated negatively. Job turnover by itself was quite unrelated to the issue of faculty status.

Ang and Koh (1997) examined the literature on job satisfaction and user information satisfaction to see if there is sufficient evidence to suggest that the 2 constructs are correlated. The factors which affect job satisfaction are similar to those which affect user information satisfaction. Examining user information satisfaction and job satisfaction in isolation would not be rigurous because the effects of relevant contextual variables have to be taken into account. Identifies the relevant contextual variables, and develops a comprehensive framework which allows investigation of the relationship between the 2 constructs. Tests the framework with a small scale study.

Beena and Poudval (1998) studied job satisfaction of two groups : Library professionals and Research and Development Personnel of Cochin University of Science and Technology. The study focused on the intrinsic (content) factors and extrinsic (context) factors. They reported that there is no significant difference in the overall job satisfaction of the two groups. The result was that content factors are more important for R&D personnel whereas for library professionals, context factors are more important.

Eden and Lawal (1999) Reported that the survey data was used to determine the influence of job satisfaction on the publication output of librarians in Nigerian universities. The results of the empirical analysis indicate that of the 6 dimensions of job satisfaction used in the study, only 3 (librarians' levels of satisfaction with their achievement, responsibility and recognition) had a significant influence on their publication output. Other dimensions including salary, university library policies and administration, and supervision, had no significant influence on their publication output.

Barlett (2000) presents a literature review of the factors of job satisfaction and describes a survey administered to 263 employees of the Wake Country Library System in North Carolina in which five communication behaviors were tested to determine their relationship to subordinate's job satisfaction. Findings indicate that four of the five offers of help, offers of cooperation, frequency of contact and trust were substantially related to subordinate's job satisfaction. Personal self disclosure was not found to be substantially related, although its task focused dimension was related to subordinate's job satisfaction.

Onohwakpor (2003) carried on a study to investigate the staff relationship among senior and junior staff in Delta State University Library ABRAKA. Data was collected from two campuses of university library by distributing 150 questionnaires to the staff. Factors associated with nature of job, staff working relationship, prospects and rewards, participation, coworkers etc. were covered in this study. The results of this survey shows that seventy percent staff in the library was satisfied with their work and working conditions, interaction between them and their boss, degree of cooperation and friendliness among staff. Thirty percent library staff showed dissatisfaction with their work, working conditions, relationship with their boss. They showed no cooperation by their co-workers in handling work load.

3.2 WOMEN LIBRARIANS AND JOB SATISFACTION

D'Elia (1979) seeks to identify the factors which are most highly related to job satisfaction. This study concentrated on librarians both males and females from Rutgers, Columbia and Drexel universities. Data collection instruments were the Minnesota Important Questionnaire for measuring vocational needs, the Minnesota Job Description Questionnaire for measuring job expectations. Analysis of variance, factor analysis and step-wise multiple regression analysis were his statistical techniques. His findings were that need gratification and expectation fulfillment were independent of each other. Further, expectation fulfillment was not related to job satisfaction. Need gratification was related to job satisfaction.

The analysis of data revealed no meaningful pattern of difference in the degree of job satisfaction experienced by public or technical services librarians, no systematic relationship between vocational needs of the librarians and their degree of job satisfaction and no significant difference in levels of job satisfaction of men and women contrary to the findings of Wahba. But there was a strong systematic relationship between the job satisfaction of the librarians and the characteristics of the job environments in which they worked.

Chopra (1984) studied job satisfaction among librarians of Lucknow city under the dimensions as work, social recognition, pay scales and promotion avenues. A significant higher percentage of female librarians were satisfied with the social status of their job and their work. A higher percentage librarians working in the social libraries were satisfied with their working conditions, pay scales and avenues for promotion. The result showed and analysed the main source of dissatisfaction especially regarding females.

Navalani (1984) surveyed "job satisfaction in relation to manpower management in university libraries of India". She took ten dimensions of job satisfaction as career, work, library practices, working conditions, supervision, communication, salary, promotion, user services and status. She collated that majority of library professionals were satisfied with their work and there was no significant difference in overall level of job satisfaction between males and females, senior and juniors indicated significant differences out of ten dimensions. Only five namely career, work, library practice, salary and promotion emerged with significant differences for both groups. She also suggested a fair deal in work pattern, to fair sex, more in-service training, reanalysis and redesigning of jobs for better utilization of human resources, more internal motivation and improvement in quality of work performance.

Rockman (1984) randomly surveyed tenure track faculty and librarians both male and female employed by the California State University System. She tested a new theory of job satisfaction among 280 academic librarians while investigating job satisfaction among faculty and librarians : A study of gender autonomy and decision-making opportunity. She found that there was a positive relationship between job satisfaction and gender but that gender alone could not be viewed as a predictor of job satisfaction. He also advocated that job satisfaction was not only solely a function of gender and membership in a dominant work group, rather it was highly correlated with autonomy and opportunities of exercise of decision-making skills.

Nazotta (1985) also made a study of the factors associated with job satisfaction of eighty male and eighty female librarians of Nigeria by adopting Minnesota Satisfaction Questionnaire (MSQ) consisting of 20 item question which measured 20 dimensions of job satisfaction and the responses to these items were made on a Likert type scale of a maximum 5 points. The study found that in a developing country where male librarians out numbered female librarians, women were more satisfied than men.

Navalani (1990) in her work on job characteristics of librarians as satisfiers reputed that majority of the librarians are satisfied with most of the attributes of their work. She found that there was difference between the perceptions of seniors and juniors, male and female staff. She also found that the female staff need more fair deal, more attention and motivation for in-service training to improve the quality of work life and to acquirc fruitful results.

Banks (1991) who carried out experiments with university women library assistants in England supports the view of (Thapisa, 1991) that pay is the most important motivator for casual workers who generally do not work full time, have only a partial psychological commitment to the organization and have no career notions. She found that a pay increase across the board rather than pay tied to goals was the most effective motivator.

Mirfakhrai (1991) studied job satisfaction in small and medium sized academic libraries in U.S. and found no significant relationship between the sex of forty eight male and seventy one female academic librarians and their overall job satisfaction.

Thapisa (1991) survey of full time women library assistants with at least two year's continuous experience in England also found lack of promotional opportunities high on the list of causes of dissatisfaction. Sixty eight percent felt that they were in dead-end jobs with no promotion prospects and nothing to work towards. Very little was done to encourage women library assistants to take up higher qualifications leading to feelings of low esteem and unimportance. The greatest source of dissatisfaction was pay. The most prevalent feeling was that library assistants should be paid more since they were the ones that kept the library running.

Thornton (2000) identified the satisfaction and dissatisfaction for 136 librarians of African descent. The data collected from the ninety nine female and thirty males regarding satisfaction in twenty three aspects of their jobs indicated that men were more satisfied than women. Although the findings tend to support Wahba's conclusion that women are more dissatisfied than men are, the differences may not be very significant. The results of this study is to examine job satisfaction of African female descent employed academic libraries holding membership in the Association of Reference Libraries (ARL). The study found that job satisfaction is critical to the retention and recruitment of librarians. It also identifies the areas & satisfaction and dissatisfaction for this group of female librarians. There has been no significant gain in the number of librarians of African descent in the ARL academic libraries in the past ten years. If libraries are to recruit and retain a diverse workforce, consideration must be given to what makes these employees remain on the job and in the same profession.

Thornton (2001) made a job satisfaction study of ninety eight female African American (Black) librarians employed in seventy nine academic libraries. The dependent variables she used are race, age, experience and duration at the present institution regarding their isolation, social discrimination and diversity programmes. She found out that the combination of gender and race made black women the least satisfied librarians. She found that there was no significant correlations between job satisfaction and the number of years in the present job.

Aina (2004) studied leadership potential of women librarians in the university libraries in Nigeria, Ghana and Sierra Leone. 210 questionnaires were sent to all the women librarians of West Africa. The questions sought to know their motivating strategies, team building attitudes, leadership attitudes and potentials and evidence of discrimination against women as leaders. Scoring system was used to analysis of data obtained by the respondents. The leadership potential of women librarians covered by this study has been investigated and their leadership skills also have been evaluated. The findings revealed that their leadership potentials and skills are satisfactory and are of good standing. The study resulted that women librarians in West Africa are effective and efficient as library administrators.

3.3 MOTIVATION AND JOB SATISFACTION

Plate and Stone (1974) conducted a study to test Herzberg theory of motivation and hygiene factors. The data was collected from 162 American and 75 Canadian librarians attending different workshops. They confirm that the theory was applicable to librarians as to other occupations, on which Herzberg et al based their conclusion. They found that motivators (factors which produced job satisfaction) were distinct from hygienes (the factors which denote job dissatisfaction). They found that motivators were concerned mainly with job content-work process factors while the hygiene factors were primarily related to the context in which the job was done, i.e. environment.

Wahba (1975) studied twenty New York based academic libraries. She investigated the sources of job satisfaction and dissatisfaction and relationship between job satisfaction and work motivation/ job performance and willingness of leave. Data was collected by the job descriptive inventry (JDI), the self-rating report of job performance developed by Porter and Lawyer, Patchen's self rating scale of motivation and the ability-willingness to leave scale. Her findings were that librarians were extremely dissatisfied with pay scales and promotion. Work was ranked as the highest source of satisfaction and satisfaction with work is highly correlated with motivation. Correlation with job satisfaction and job performance were not conclusive.

Wahba (1978) studied job satisfaction of librarians working in academic libraries of New York Metropolitan Areas. She investigated the source of job satisfaction and dissatisfaction of librarians and relationship between job satisfaction and work motivation/job performance and willingness to leave. Her findings were that librarians were extremely dissatisfied with pay scales and promotion. Work was ranked as the highest source of satisfaction, and satisfaction with work was highly correlated with motivation.

Khanna (1981) conducted a survey on motivation of university librarians. Maslow's theory of hierarchy of needs, Herzberg's two factor theory of motivation and Vroom's Expectancy Valence model of motivation are the basis of the work. 240 respondents from 28 university libraries located in 19 places from the sample. His hypothesis that: 1. The choice of library profession as a career would be proceeded by a vocational growth process. 2. People already in the library profession would be advising their children/ kith and kin to adopt librarianship as a career.

Work efficient would be related to both intrinsic and extrinsic motivating factors. For collecting the data, he used three tools, Work Efficiency Scale (WERS), Maslow Security-Insecurity Inventory (SII) and Structured Interview Schedule (SIS). The results did not support the first hypothesis, rejected the second hypothesis and highlighted that there was a strong correlation between motivational factors and work efficiency. The study suggested no investigations on the study.

Kapoor (1982) made a survey of motivation among professional library staff with special reference to librarians of University of Delhi Library System and determined job characteristics which are well known motivational factors like salary, promotional avenues, facilities for higher education and in-service training, job security, autonomy in work, recognition of performance and participation in decision-making.

McNally (1983) carried out research in 1980-81 of job satisfaction among reference staff in the public library systems in Ontario library regions, and covered 10 libraries in 3 regions. 81 responded. The results revealed generally moderate satisfaction with environmental conditions but low motivation. The initial hypothesis that professionals would express greater motivation and satisfaction than non-professionals, was not confirmed. He concluded that they were of average competence, enjoyed their work and colleagues and experienced high job satisfaction despite being poorly paid and having little opportunity for advancement or participation in the administration of their libraries.

Goulding (1995) reported the results of a study which reviewed the literature relating to the position and job satisfaction of library support staff which presented some of the results of an interview based survey of such staff carried out in 9 UK public libraries during 1992. Focuses specifically on questions asked about why the respondents chose library work, and what they found satisfying or unsatisfying about their current jobs. Working with the public was the highest rated satisfaction aspect : 21 per cent of respondents were unable to think of anything dissatisfying about their job. A majority of those who could felt the most disagreeable aspect was the inability to provide as good a service as they would have liked. Excessive workload and lack of opportunities for advancement came next, rated equally.

Mahavir Singh (1995) while studying the job motivation of library professionals in relation to organizational climate and personal characteristics found job factors more effective than institutional climate or personal or familial needs on tradition. Similarly demographic factors were also projected as weak agents of motivation. It was further reported that strong job involvement does not seem to be generating from inside but it seems to be thrusting upon from outside.

Hall (1999) reported results of a questionnaire survey, based on an MA thesis, Sheffield university, department of information studies, of 98 UK public library staff within a single library authority to determine the causes of job dissatisfaction and absenteeism. Results indicated that physical working conditions and salary levels provoked the most dissatisfaction and that library assistants tended to be dissatisfied with their working relationship with professionally qualified colleagues. Examination of absence records over several years showed that, although colds and viral infections accounted for 43 per cent of illnesses they only accounted for 26.4 per cent of the total number of days lost. Conversely, stress, anxiety and depression accounted for 2.8 per cent of the recorded absences but 15.8 per cent of the time lost.

Sanghi (2001) conducted a study to investigate the motivational climate in relation to job satisfaction and organizational commitment of employees in the workshop of one of railway units.

Ustun (2002) conducted a study in the information centres (libraries, archives and information-documentation centres) of Istanbul (Turkey). The purpose of this study is to investigate the relationship between job satisfaction and productivity by comparing the employees of two institutions which differ in their organization i.e. the state university libraries and the privately endowed university libraries with their greater rewards and motivating factors and to draw conclusions based on the significant variables. The questionnaire was administered to a total of 185 librarians in twenty main university libraries and their affiliated units. Organisation of data to bring it into some meaningful order was done by hand. Tables were created on the computer using the Excel program. The study reported that young people seek a higher degree of motivating factors than aged people in maximum variables.

In this study, the theoretical foundations of job satisfaction and productivity are first considered then, within this theoretical framework, an applied study is made of all university libraries in Istanbul. These libraries, which exhibit two different styles of administration (the state university library and the private endowed university library) also differ significantly in term of the motivating factors they offer their employees. The hypothesis is that job satisfaction has a beneficial effect on productivity, job satisfaction and dedication to work among employees of these two different institutions are examined and compared on the basis of data obtained by the survey method.

3.4 STRESS AND JOB SATISFACTION

Chrisman (1975) in his dissertation compared job related tension, job satisfaction and group cohesiveness of different groups of librarians, viz. cataloguers, reference librarians and other professional librarians. His hypothesis was that there was no difference between the self perception of cataloguers and that of other two groups in regard to role consensus relating to position, role ambiguity, role pressure, job satisfaction and group cohesiveness. His study was based on the population of two university libraries. He included all available professional librarians. The three instruments used for collecting data were: Kahn's Job Related Tension Index, Brayfield's and Rothe's Job Satisfaction Index and Seashero's Group Cohesiveness Index.

Prasad and Singh (1990) showed results of a study of fifty libraries of the Central Library Banaras Hindu University which aimed to investigate job anxiety in relation to job satisfaction which the individual derives from various aspects of job life. Results revealed that as job anxiety scores increased, job satisfaction indices decreased. The more anxious an employee is about the various dimensions of his/her job, the less satisfaction he/she is with his/her job life.

Schneider (1991) compared levels and sources of

stress and job satisfaction of public service and technical service employees in a large urban public library system.

Pollard (1995) stated organizational stress re-utilized activities that contribute to profitability, professionalism stresses ethical performance that contributes to social responsibility. When the organization prevails, autonomy, authority, and control, the hallmarks of professionalism, weaken. This leads to a decrease in the intrinsic meaning of work and, ultimately, less job satisfaction. Using a stratified random national sample, these assumptions were explored among Canadian news workers. More professionalism, a less formal and smaller organization, media sector and several social attributes lead to more job satisfaction. Newspaper workers were most satisfied due to a combination of intrinsic factors, such as autonomy, authority, and control of work, and extrinsic factors, such as job security and income.

Raza and Gupta (2000) reported the findings of research on library professionals working in DULS. The study is an attempt to measure the extent of job satisfaction and effect of job anxiety and the relationship among library professionals according to their position in the library hierarchy. Job content, management, personal adjustment and social relations areas were covered. Seven dimensions as security, recognition, human relations at work, reward and punishment, self esteem, future prospects and capacity to work were studied. Analysed that majority of library professionals were satisfied in four areas covered.

Awasthi (2002) conducted doctorate research on stress and burn out among library professional staff in the colleges and universities of Punjab, Haryana and Chandigarh. She found that the lower staff was more satisfied with their work. She proved that there exists a significant difference between library professionals grouped on the basis of their designations and status. She also reported that good personal relations among the staff had positive influence on their work, culture and dedication.

Haridasan and Sultan (2002) studied occupational stress and burn out among library staff of Gorakpur University and the thirteen factors causing stress. The factors under study were role overload, role ambiguity, role conflict, poor peer relations, working conditions, low status etc. Result revealed that librarians are under stress. Professional assistants showed under participation and stressful working conditions. Role ambiguity among junior professional assistants was responsible for their stress. In semi-professionals, the stress was due to their role conflict. Deputy librarians had higher degree of burnout where among the labour staff, there is less degree of burnout.

Sornam and Sudha (2003) studied the level of Occupational Role Stress (ORS) among women library professionals working in colleges of Bharathidasen. The study identified the certain demographic variables like age, experience, qualification and marital status and their relationship with ORS. The findings were that there was significant difference and relationship between the different demographic variables and had significant association with ORS.

3.5 DEMOGRAPHICS AND JOB SATISFACTION

Scamell (1980) examined the relationship of age and tenure of job satisfaction. The sample comprised sixty four U.S. professional librarians. The findings indicated that the librarians studied experienced relatively constant levels of job satisfaction across three different age and tenure categories. The primary job satisfaction noted related to age and satisfaction with supervision and co-workers.

Garg (1986) carried out a study in India with the purpose to assess job satisfaction of librarians of universities of Delhi and Rajasthan. The study had the following objectives: 1. To measure and compare personal background personality and job satisfaction of librarians. 2. To determine the significant correlation of job satisfaction 3. To find out the partial correlation between personality and job satisfaction, between personal background and job satisfaction 4. To determine the multiple correlation of the combined effect of personal background and personality with job satisfaction and 5. To offer recommendation for improvement of job satisfaction.

Study comprised professional seniors, professional juniors, documentation officers, professional assistants, senior technical assistants drawn from six university libraries situated in Rajasthan and Delhi. The self designed personal data form was used to gather data regarding eleven personal background factors, i.e. age, sex, marital status, qualification, occupational level, present tenure etc. The long form version of Minnesota Satisfaction Questionnaire (MSQ) designed at the industrial relations centre of University of Minnesota was used to measure the degree of job satisfaction experienced by librarians.

Lynch and Verdin (1987) replicated the study which was conducted in 1983 entitled job satisfaction in the work setting, reached a similar conclusion. The findings were that old workers and more experienced workers were more satisfied than younger and less experienced persons. Supervision, co-workers, communication, promotion, benefits and pay were covered. Demographic variables as area of work, age, sex, work with patrons, full time, part-time and library size were covered.

Alao (1992) reported findings of a survey of 54 library assistants in 4 Nigerian academic institutions using the Minnesota Satisfaction Questionnaire in order to determine the degree of job satisfaction experienced. Results were analysed in terms of the following demographic variables : age; sex; marital status; length of service in library; length of service in the present section; level of education; and departmental affiliation.

Sangam, et al (1996) carried out a study of job satisfaction of twenty libraries of Karnataka University and its colleges. The findings were that there was no relation between length of service and job satisfaction. Gender, age, and marital status has no relation with job satisfaction. They also found that librarians have failed to understand the importance of autonomy and self-actualisation.

Garg (1999) reported relationship of personal background aspects, two dimensions of personality and twenty aspects of job satisfaction with general job satisfaction of professional librarians, employed in three university libraries of Delhi. Personal background factors were age, sex, marital status, qualification, present tenure, past tenure etc. Personality dimensions include neuroticism and extraversion. Twenty job factors pertaining to specific factors of job as work, supervision, independence, policies, coworkers etc. The findings were that there was significant relationship between personal factors, personality factors and specific job factors with general job satisfaction.

Landry (2000) discusses the importance of job satisfaction for library staff working at the reference desk. It not only affects their quality of life and the overall level of life satisfaction experienced by the reference staff, it also affects the quality of reference work itself. Satisfied employees maintain attitudes and engage in activities conducive to reference service effectiveness. Life satisfaction and job satisfaction are related in a reciprocal manner, with life satisfaction having the strong effect. Reports results of a study which found a moderate positive relationship between life satisfaction and job satisfaction. A moderate negative relationship was found between life satisfaction and the desire to find a comparable job in another library. Discusses the practical implications for library directors, educators in the field of library and information science and librarians.

Williamson and others (2005) collected data on personality characteristics, job satisfaction and career satisfaction from more than 1300 informational professionals. Respondents included academic reference librarians, archivists, cataloguers, distance education librarians, public librarians, records managers, school media specialists, special librarians, system librarians and other information professionals who responded to requests or picked up questionnaires at a national library conference. Significant correlations were obtained between personality variables and both career and job satisfaction. Step-wise regression analysis were performed, revealing the five variables (optimism, emotional stability, teamwork, visionary work style and work drive) accounted for 20% of variance in job satisfaction. Four variables accounted for 19% of the variance in career satisfaction (optimism, work drive, emotional resilience and assertiveness).

Hierarchical regression analysis were performed to test Lounsbury et-al's general composite measure of emotional resilience, work drive and optimism as predictors of job and career satisfaction. These variables accounted for 18% of the variance in job satisfaction and 19% of variance in career satisfaction. Recommendations for employees to help with hiring and managing information professionals were made.

3.6 PARTICIPATIVE MANAGEMENT & JOB SATISFACTION

Marchant (1970) studied job satisfaction as one of the five development variables in his dissertation. He attempted to find out the applicability of Rensis Likert's Participative Management theory to university libraries. Profile of organization characteristics was used for measurement of variables. The questionnaire which he administered to professional staff working in 22 university libraries, for collecting the data containing questions pertaining to job satisfaction. Staff scores on overall satisfaction were used in analyzing the effect of participative decision-making on satisfaction. The techniques of the research were that participation of librarians in the decision-making process and participative style of management within librarians improved job satisfaction of librarians.

Horenstein (1993) examinerd job satisfaction of academic library staff as it relates to faculty status and participation of librarians in library planning and decision-making, university academic affairs and professional library activities. A questionnaire survey was carried out covering 300 US academic librarians at a random sample of universities and colleges in USA with enrolments exceeding 2,000 students. An SPSS (Statistical Package for the Social Sciences) data analysis of 638 responses focused on job satisfaction of three groups of librarians : librarians with no faculty status or rank, librarians with either faculty status or rank but not both; and librarians with both faculty status and rank. Academic librarians with both faculty status and rank were more satisfied than librarians in other two groups. They also perceived themselves as more involved in library planning and decision-making, more frequently consulted, better informed about.

Leckie and Brett (1997) report results of a questionnaire survey of university libraries in Canda which investigated the job satisfaction of Canadian University librarians and which replicated the techniques used by Horenstein's U.S. Study (1993) so as to facilitate international comparisons. The study explored the relationships between academic status, administration and the participation of librarians in library planning and decision making, university affairs and professional activities. Data anlaysis concentrated on comparisons between academic status librarians and non-academic status librarians, and between administrative librarians and non-administration librarians. Although academic status librarians were significantly more satisfied with their involvement in university affairs, promotion and tenure processes, they were not more satisfied with other dimensions of their work such as work load and salary. Administrative librarians, on the other hand were significantly more satisfied with most of the major aspects of work being measured, and perceived themselves to be much more involved in library planning and university affairs than non-administrative librarians.

3.7 INFORMATION TECHNOLOGY AND JOB SATISFACTION

Woodruff (1980) collected data of 202 data processing personnel by Minnesota Satisfaction Questionnaire (MSQ). Comparisons of twenty job satisfaction dimensions of these personnel with studies of accountants and engineers utilizing the same instrument, revealed that satisfaction with advancement and compensation was particularly low. Operations personnel reported lower job satisfaction that the other functional groups of the data processing personnel. It also reviews the studies conducted on job satisfaction in USA till now.

Waters (1988) studied job satisfaction in the light of new technology developments in a university library and dug out prestige, self esteem and social relations as positive factors of job satisfaction.

Estabrook and Bird (1990) conducted a study to determine whether automation made a difference in job satisfaction of professional and support staff in one private and three public university libraries in order to investigate the factors that contributed significantly to job satisfaction; whether use of technology related significantly to job satisfaction and staff likes and dislikes. He found that among professional librarians were more satisfied than black librarians. This finding is disturbing, for it suggests that libraries do not treat minority workers equally.

Morita (1991) while recognizing that increased sophistication in online Public Access Catalog (OPACs) with keyword searching has diminished the importance of subject heading searches and that library catalogues are now supplemented on-line by catalogues of other libraries and other bibliographical data bases, finds an expanding role for cataloguers. Cataloguers are now able to utilize their skills in a variety of ways, including educating users to use catalogue more effectively and in advising libraries how to provide optimal access to a variety of bibliographic (and textual) information. The cataloguers find new opportunities to expand their role into public service, educational, and technical areas not previously possible.

Whitlatch (1991) reviews the literature dealing with job satisfaction among library reference staff and its relationship with job performance. Studies of the role played by the computerization of library systems on employee job satisfaction lead to the conclusion that stress might prove a better focus than job satisfaction. Indicates ways in which the reference librarians work can bc designed to reduce stress by the introduction of computers.

Zeffene (1994) examines the impact of computer usage on job satisfaction based on a survey of 1300 employees from the Australian Telecommunications Industry. Results show that job satisfaction is positively influenced by the extent of computer use, aspects of computer related training and demographic characteristics such as tenure and job position. However, by catering for different areas of computer use and by controlling job position and tenure, finds that use in different functional areas tends to affect user satisfaction to a different degree. It uncovers personnel and training issues that organizations involved in extensive computerization may need to address.

Barker (1995) stated that end user computing is an information technology that has emerged to enable users to address for themselves information needs that otherwise would not be met. The impact that this technology has on the job users performance has not been addressed. Research in end user computing states that this technology is a user driven phenomenon that users enthuiastically embrance, yet an examination of the studies in office automation, which as a technology is very similar to end user computing, report mostly negative reactions to the technology. The answer to this difference may lie in the nature of the addition of further skills to the job. Prior research has shown that end user computing does add content to their users' content to jobs as well. Examines whether increasing complexity in end user computing activity will lead to perceived increases in job motivation and job satisfaction. Categorizes users by their end user computing activity, and finds that these levels of sue are associated with certain job and increased job satisfaction.

Sadeh and Sycara (1995) contributed to a special volume on planning and scheduling and artificial intelligence. Studies a version of the job shop scheduling problem in which some operations have to be scheduled within non relaxable time windows. This problem is a well know NP-complete constraint satisfaction problem (CSP). A popular method for solving this type of problems involves using depth first back track search. Earlier work focused on the development of consistency enforcing techniques and variable/value ordering heuristics that improve the efficiency of this search procedure. Combines these techniques with new look back schemes that help the search procedure recover from so called dead end search states. Describes 3 intelligent backtracking schemes: Dynamic Consistency Enforcement dynamically identifies critical subproblems and determines how far to backtrace by selectively enforcing higher levels of consistency among variables participating in these critical subproblems; learning ordering from failure dynamically modifies the order in which variables are instantiated based on earlier conflicts; and incomplete back jumping heuristic abandons areas of the search space that appear to require excessive computational efforts. These schemes are shown to : further reduce the average complexity of the backtrack search procedure, enable the system to efficiency solve problems that could not be solved otherwise due to excessive computation cost, and be more effective at solving job shop scheduling problems than other look-back schemes advocated in the literature.

Stamm and Underwood (1995) who reported about a survey of 187 editors at 13 Northwest America newspaper found that computer pagination software is not responsible for widespread anger and unhappiness in newsroom. Pagination makes both positive and negative contributions to job satisfaction. Most of the editors still took pride in their newspapers and found editing satisfying despite changes.

Pascoe (1996) reports the findings of a research study carried out in large Australian Research Library in Canberra which investigated the impact on job satisfaction of introducing an integrated information management system. The job diagnostic survey formed the largest part of the data collection instrument used in the study. Results indicated that a number of factors may influence job satisfaction when such technology introduced into the work place : Workers expected concerns over health and safety issues; social satisfaction and perceptions that their skills may have become devalued by the new system.

Geeson and Goulding (1999) reported the findings of a study investigating the job satisfaction of learning centre support staff at a multi site university, focusing on whether differences in satisfaction existed at different sites. Using qualities research methods, assistants across the 5 learning centre sites of the university were interviewed The results showed that good customer relations, work variety and challenge were satisfying, while problems with the computer network, lack of consultation and lack of interaction between the staff at different sites were dissatisfying. Draws conclusions and makes suggestions to managers.

4

Research Methodology and Procedure

"Irrationally held truths may be more harmful than reasoned error." — ***Thomas H. Huxley***

4.1 RESEARCH

Research is an absorbing, exciting, enjoyable and hopefully, enormously productive activity. It is a systematic process of collecting and analyzing information (data) in order to increase our understanding of the phenomenon with which we are concerned or interested.

Research is not more information gathering. A fourth-grade child comes from school with this saying/ announcement. "Mom, the teacher sent us to the library today to do research, and I learned a lot about "Columbus". The child has been given the idea that research means going to the library to get information discovery; it may be learning reference skills; but it certainly is not, as the teacher so termed it, research (Jain, 2005, p. 2-3).

Research is considered to be formal, systematic and intensive process of carrying on scientific method of analysis (Best and Kahn, 1986, p.12). It is an objective attempt to study a problem for deriving general purpose.

Research means advancement of science and knowledge. Research is systematic inquiry to discover new facts/data or relations between them by objective methods. It is a problem solving approach. Research is an intellectual act that starts with the asking of a questions and progress through the critical and analytical study of evidence and arrives at new conclusions or new knowledge.

Webster's New International Dictionary (1981, p. 1930) defines research as:

"A studious enquiry or examination; specifically and usually. Critical and exhaustive investigation or experimental having for its aim the discovery of new facts and their correct interpretation, the revision of accepted conclusions, theories or laws in the light of newly discovered facts or practical applications of new or revised conclusions, theories or laws."

Research of any kind is a careful investigation through search for new facts in society. Social research is defined as "Systematic method of discovery new facts or verifying old facts, their sequences, interrelationship, causal explanations and the natural laws which govern them." (Prabhakar, 2001, p.1).

Research is a diligent, careful and exhaustive investigation of a specific subject matter, having as its aim the advancement of mankind's knowledge (Sharma, 2007, p. 2).

Singh (2002, p.3) stated research as "a rational process which enables a research to arrive-at dependable solution to problems using planned and systematic approach."

Now, it is a saying that research is purposive, scientific and pointed deliberation. It is necessary to adopt and evolve a systematic method to collect essential data.

After selection, definition and delimitation of the problem, the adoption of suitable measures becomes imperative. Since research is not a haphazard task, it requires one to proceed in a definite direction along with all defined lines. Collection of more bits of information is not research. Planning and selection of a method is very essential to collect factual material relevant data, unknown and untapped so far, adequate in quality and quantity to save it from becoming heap of jumbled ideas gathered from here and there. So, the ultimate success of the research project greatly depends upon the method employed therein.

In social scientific research, it is necessary to understand the difference between method and methodology.

4.2 METHOD

By method, we mean a systematic approach towards particular phenomena. It denotes a procedure, tool or technique used by the researcher to generate data, analyse data or both on the basis of empirical observations and logical reasoning.

Goode and Hatt (1952, p.35) state that, scientific method is the gateway to explore the truth, verifiability, generality, predictability, and objectivity, systematically are the characteristics of the scientific methods. Burgess (1985, p.1) describes that, the term method is little more that an outline of techniques which can be used by the researcher.

4.3 RESEARCH METHODOLOGY

Research methodology is logic of scientific investigation. Methodology means description, explanation and justification of methods (Dabas, 2001, p. 113).

Kothari (1999, p.1) observed that methodology in practice lays down the procedures and steps that are generally adopted by a researcher in studying the research problem. These procedures are justified by means of scientific observations. He concluded that the primary objective of all research is "Search for Knowledge."

In a research, there are numerous methods and procedures to be applied. But it is the nature of problem under investigation which determines the adoption of a particular method and procedure. So, methods, procedures and techniques differ according to the problem and availability of time (Gupta, 2006, p.18). Research methodology helps the investigator to carefully plan the steps taken in the research process.

4.3.1. Various Research Methodologies

There are many types of research methodologies i.e. qualitative and quantitative, normative survey, field working inductive, positivist and grounded theory etc.

To attack the problem for present study comprehensively and by keeping in mind the objectives of the study and the type of data required, the investigator adopted survey method that may elicit the degree of satisfaction from the subjects (Women Librarians).

4.3.1.1. Survey Research

The word survey means "to look over" or "to oversee". Thus, observation is the main thing in survey.

Survey testing is relatively more scientific and accurate and provides more accurate data. It is a descriptive type of research that describes situations, events, systems and structures etc. Survey method provides information of:

- What exists
- What we want
- And how to get that

Survey research is directed towards ascertaining the prevailing conditions. It seeks to answer the questions like; what are the real facts with regard to the existing practices and conditions (Good and Scates, 1954, p. 40).

Survey research is present oriented research. It is the art and science of asking questions or observing behaviour to obtain information. It is one of the most important areas of measurement in applied social research.

Survey method in which data is gathered from a relatively large number of cases at a particular time. It involves a clearly defined problem and definite objectives, keeping in view the objectives and purpose of the research and availability of instrument.

In the words of Tull and Albaum (1973, p.2), "Survey research is the systematic gathering of information from (a sample or full population) respondents for the purpose of understanding or predicting some aspect of the behaviour of the population of interest." Survey may be descriptive, comparative and evaluative.

The broad area of survey research encompasses any measurement procedures that involve asking questions of respondents. A "Survey" can be of any form a short paper-and-pencil feedback from an intensive one-on-one indepth interview. Surveys are roughly divided into two broad areas: Questionnaires and interviews. In simple, a survey is a critical inspection, often official to provide exact information.

4.3.1.2. Questionnaire

Sommer and Sommer (1986, p.197) state that, a questionnaire is a structured series of written questions on a topic about which the respondents' opinions are sought, in survey research the systematic gathering of information about people's beliefs, attitude, values and behavior.

Regarding data collection, the most popular method in a survey research is questionnaire method. Questionnaires are usually paper-and-pencil instruments that the respondents completes (Jain, 2005, p.156).

It is a written document, listing a series of questions pertaining to a problem under study to which the investigator requires answers. It may be defined as a data gathering devices containing a list of logically arranged written questions on a problem under investigation (Singh, 2002, p.12).

4.3.1.3. Interview

Next to questionnaire method, most of the surveys are made on personal interviews which allow a high response rate, direct interaction between the surveyor and the surveyed; clarification of questions and elaboration of data through the minimization of unclear answers is conceptually the superior form of study technique.

Interview is a better form of research than questionnaire. But the primary drawback of personal interview is the longer time involvement even in a sample population of moderate size (Samantaray, 1998, p.33).

The observation method is also very time consuming and it has been seen that at times the subjects do not allow to be observed. And while observing, the scholar can become subjective.

4.4 RESEARCH DESIGN FOR THE PRESENT STUDY

To attack the problem for present study comprehensively and by keeping in mind the objectives of the study and the type of data required, the investigator's choice automatically fell on "Survey Mcthod" that may elicit the degree of satisfaction on job from the subjects (Women Librarians).

The present research entitled "Job Satisfaction Among Women Library Professionals working in the universities and colleges of Punjab" falls mainly within the perview of Survey Research Design. Survey research studies large and small population by selecting samples chosen from the population to discover the relative incidence, distribution and interrelations of sociological and psychological variables and are best used focusing on people at work, the vital facts of people, their attitude towards their job satisfaction, motivational level and other behavioural aspects. It throws useful light on the various aspects of social problems and helps in understanding the existing problems and the mutual interplay of causes.

It requires careful analysis, interpretation of data gathered and logical and skillful reporting of the findings.

4.5 RESEARCH METHODOLOGY FOR THE PRESENT STUDY

Designing of a good research project always depends upon the choice of the sample as well as a defined methodology for both collection and interpretation of data.

The problem in hand has been conducted by adopting the following research methodology and it has been categorized in the following folds for the ease of discussion.

1. Locale of the study
2. Selection of sample area and sample size.
3. Sampling technique.
4. Selection of the tool and technique.
5. Constructing of the tool.
6. Pilot study
7. Collection of data
8. Data processing
9. Statistical techniques used
10. Scheme of the work (Chapterization)

4.5.1. Locale of the Study

The present study covers the area of state of Punjab and its various universities and colleges. The number of respondents being large, the sample has been made representative of different districts, universities and types of colleges.

Place of research is Amritsar.

4.5.2. Sample Area

India is a vast country having more than 550 universities and a large number of colleges affiliated to these universities. It is not possible to cover all of them. So, the present study is limited to the women library professionals working in universities and colleges of the state of Punjab including Chandigarh. It is hoped that the results obtained will be applicable to other regions of the country also. Hence, following universities and their affiliated colleges form the basis of the present study:

1. Guru Nanak Dev University, Amritsar.
2. Punjab Agricultural University, Ludhiana.
3. Punjab Technical University, Jalandhar.
4. Panjab University, Chandigarh.
5. Punjabi University, Patiala

4.5.3. Sample Size

This investigation is restricted to womcn library processionals in these universities and their colleges. Already action of Dr. Ranganathan classified the library professional staff into four broader categories: Professionals (Librarians); Professional Seniors (Deputy Librarians); Professional Juniors (Assistant Librarians); and Professional Assistants (Library Assistants, Library Restorers and Attendants).

So, Library professionals include category of Librarians, Deputy Librarians, Assistant Librarians, Professional Assistants includes Library Assistants, Library Restorers / Library Attendants.

The present study involved 200 women library professionals from university and college libraries of Punjab and Chandigarh. Women librarians having permanent posts with different designations possess professional qualifications from minimum to maximum (i.e. Diploma/Certificate Course Holders, B.Lib. SC, M.Lib. Sc, .M.Phil and even Ph.D.) in library science. The respondents having professional experience more than three years have been included in the sample. The questionnaires were delivered personally and the respondents were requested to fill the answers on the spot. So, the investigator included all those professionals in the study who were available and willing to cooperate. Some respondents promised to send the filled questionnaires by post but some of them never obliged despite requests on phone.

4.6 Sampling Technique

Sampling is a process of selecting a subset of randomized number of members of the population of a study and collecting data about their attributes. The limited members of the population selected for sampling are called as sampling units. Based on the data at the sample, the analyst draws inference about the population.

In a statistical enquiry, when only a part of the population or only a group of units is taken into consideration, it is called a sample method of enquiry. In statistical investigations, there is a long established practice by which a part of an aggregate is selected to represent the whole universe (Ghosh, 1982, p.200).

According to New Standard Encyclopedia (1981, p.624) "A sampling method is used to discover the prevailing opinions, attitudes and beliefs of a large group of people on some question or issue.

4.6.1. Advantages

Following are main advantages of sampling:

1. Less time taken to collect data.
2. Less cost and money for data collection.
3. More accuracy of data collection due to its limited size.

4. When the number of units are scattered, sampling technique is very useful and can be conducted in a convenient way (Panneerselvam, 2007, p.191)

4.6.2. Disadvantages

1. If the method of sampling is faulty, the conclusion derived from this becomes inaccurate.
2. Specialized knowledge is required for applying sampling.
3. Phenomena of complex nature creates difficulty.
4. If the units are not homogeneous, sampling technique will be hazardous and unscientific.

4.6.3. Nature of Sampling Applied

If the units under study are geographically scattered, small sample is more suitable. If the selection of sample is done by the stratified sampling method, the reliability and accuracy can be obtained by small sized samples (Ghosh, 1982, p. 207).

By taking this point into consideration, stratified sampling method had been followed to collect data from the respondents under study and to achieve the results in accordance with the objectives and hypothesis of the study.

4.6.4. Stratified Sampling

Stratified sampling is an improvised sampling over simple random sampling and systematic sampling. This sampling has more statistical efficiency when the population is known to consist of a number of distinct categories, characteristics or demographics.

In this sampling method, the population is divided into a specified set of strata such that the members within each stratum have similar attributes but the members between stratas have dissimilar attributes.

This means that each stratum is homogeneous when compared to the population.

According to International Encyclopedia of Social Sciences (1968, p.606), "The primary aim of stratified is to increase the amount of information per unit of cost. A further aim may be to obtain adequate information about certain strata of special interest."

Simply, we can say that under this system, the universe is divided into a number of groups or stratas. Then, certain dumber of items are taken from each group of random bias.

4.7 SELECTION OF TOOLS

Included what is tool and its description

4.7.1. What is the Tool?

For collecting data required for the study of any problem, the investigator may use various devices. For each type of research, the investigator needs certain instruments in order to gather new facts or to explore new fields. The instruments thus employed as means are called "Tools".

Keeping in mind all the merits and demerits of various methodologies and in the light of the sample size considered by earlier researchers as evidenced from the published literature on the concerned study, the two tools questionnaires and interviews were made as data collection. So, the sample of 200 female librarians considered for this study seemed to be adequate for a project of this type.

Therefore, in an Indian situation, a combination of tools: Questionnaires and interviews were chosen for the present study.

Description of the Tool : included questionnaires statistics and its construction.

A questionnaire was designed and pretested by distributing among a group of women librarians. It was further improved on the basis of suggestions received by the respondents. The finalized questionnaires were then distributed among the universe of population under study.

Questionnaire Statistics

Universities Data		*Colleges Data/ colleges response = 74*
Number of universities covered	5	80
Total questionnaires distributed	90	135
Questionnaires received at the time of survey.	52	42
Questionnaires received in response to first reminder	21	32
Questionnaires received in response to second reminder	13	40
No response	4	21
Total questionnaires received	86	114
Response rate	95%	84%

Total questionnaires distributed = 225

Total questionnaires received back = 200

Total response rate = 89%

4.8 CONSTRUCTION OF THE TOOL

The questionnaire was designed in a systematic manner by following the guidelines of Satisfaction–Dissatisfaction Employees Inventory (S–D Employees Inventory) which has been developed and standardized by (Pestonjee, 1973). This inventory is based on the interaction model of job satisfaction with a number of on-the-job and off-the-job factors (Vroom, 1964). The questionnaire covered on-the job and off-the-job factors associated to job satisfaction under the specific dimensions such as:

1. Job satisfaction
2. Job situation/working environment
3. Job Motivation
4. Recruitment and Promotion Policy
5. Job and Family
6. Personal and Social Factors
7. Personal (Demographic) Data

Note: The beginning part of the questionnaire designed for present study has been presented under the title "Library Profession".

4.9 PILOT STUDY

Pilot study means small scale experiment done before the actual research. It is a set of observations undertaken to decide how and whether to launch a full scale project. Researcher prepared questionnaire for the study. The questionnaire was pretested before finally using it for survey population. The pretest questionnaires were distributed to 35 women library professionals of Bhai Gurdas Library, Guru Nanak Dev University and 15 questionnaires were distributed to the subjects under study in the eight colleges of Amritsar. So, a total of 50 questionnaires were distributed for the experimental study.

Among them, 42 questionnaires were received back. Some minor changes were made in the language, meaning and structure of questionnaire on the basis of feed back and suggestions received from the respondents. This helped to give a final shape to the questionnaire to use on the survey population.

4.10 SCORING

Scores for the questionnaires based on Satisfaction–Dissatisfation, Employees Inventory having on-the-job and off-the-job factors have been obtained by frequency percentage for each factor of questionnaire. Summation of all the scores together provided the total job satisfaction score.

4.11 DATA PROCESSING

Responses obtained were first of all codified in accordance with the data handling grammar and then processed and subjected to the statistical treatment of the computer, and with the help of Karl Pearson's Product Moment correlation coefficient(s), as well as highly sophisticated multivariate techniques which have the twin advantages of utilizing all the variables/factors under study and simultaneously identifying the impact of each independent variable on the target variable and to study the interrelationship/correlation of different variables to each other (Singh and Kumar, 2006, p.90).

4.12 STATISTICAL TREATMENT OF DATA

The multivariable techniques employed in this study are Frequency Percentage, Factor Analysis, Multiple Correlation, Stepwise Regression, Ranking, F-statistics, Mann-Whitney Non-Parametric U-test and Logistic Model.

Frequency Percentage : Since the data is very vast and in order to make it meaningful, the percentage of frequencies has been calculated

Factor Analysis has been applied to detect the most significant factors which have caused the variations in our findings.

Multiple Correlation has been applied to examine

the relationships between the different factors of job satisfaction.

Stepwise Regression has been used to identify the level of influence of variables/factors on each other. Stepwise Regression detected the impact of most significant variable(s) on our dependent variables and found how much variation is caused by an independent variable and dependent variable.

Ranking Method has been used to detect the level of job satisfaction between the different factors. Mean values of every rank associates to different factors have also been drawn which are shown in the form of bar charts.

F-statistics is used to check the significance of the difference between the variances of two populations (i.e. university women librarians and college women librarians). We set the following hypothesis for this:

Under $H_0 : \sigma_1^2 = \sigma_2^2$ i.e. variances are statistically same.

Against $H_0 : \sigma_1^2 \neq \sigma_2^2$ $H_1 : \sigma_1^2 \neq \sigma_2^2$; variances are statistically differ significantly

Mann Whitney Non-parametric U-test has been applied to test whether there is any significant difference between the perceptions about job satisfaction of the respondents (Hariharan and Ganeshan, 2003 :11).

4.13 LOGISTIC MODEL

This has been applied here because of the qualitative nature of the dependent variables.

Logistic Model Explained

To check the factor affecting job satisfaction, we have applied logistic model. The choice of logistic model has been governed by the fact that satisfaction is qualitative in nature and when the dependant variable is qualitative in nature, the traditional method of ordinary least square is not applicable. Therefore, due to the dummy (binary) nature of dependent variable, we have applied logistic model as such.

In contrast to probit model (which is based upon cumulative normal probability function), this model is based on the cumulative logistic probability function. It is not used when dependent variable involves choice. Suppose, the choice is vote or not to vote for a particular candidate. Similarly, choice may be to purchase or not to purchase a house or a scooter. In such cases, probabilities are involved. The logistic probability is stated as under:

$$P_i = \frac{1}{1+e-Z_i} \qquad \ldots (1)$$

where, $Z_i = \alpha + \beta \times i + Ui$ ... (2)

From (1) we get

$$P_i(1 + e - Z_i) = 1$$

$$1 + e^{-zi} = \frac{1}{P_i}$$

$$e^{-zi} = \frac{1}{P_i} - 1 = \frac{1-P_i}{P_i}$$

$$= \frac{1}{e^{zi}} = \frac{1-P_i}{P_i}$$

Taking reciprocals

$$= e^{zi} \frac{P_i}{1-P_i}$$

Taking log of both sides

$$\log e^{zi} = \log \frac{Pi}{1Pi}$$

$$Z_i = \log \frac{Pi}{1 - Pi} \qquad \dots (3)$$

Putting (2) in (3)

$$a + bxi + Ui = \log \frac{Pi}{1 - Pi}$$

$$\log \frac{Pi}{1 - Pi} = a + bxi + Ui \qquad \dots (4)$$

Model (4) is called logistic model.

Pi/(1-Pi) shows odds in favour of making choice i.e. the household will opt to purchase scooter. As we consider logarithm, due to this model is known as logistic model.

(Estimation of model)

Estimation of model involve some difficulties.

Suppose $Pi = 1$

In this case $\log \frac{Pi}{1 - Pi} = Pg \frac{1}{1 - 1} = \log\left(\frac{1}{0}\right) = \log(\infty)$

Which is not defined. Hence estimation is not possible when

$Pi = 1$

Suppose $Pi = 0$

$$\log \frac{Pi}{1 - Pi} = \log\left(\frac{0}{1 - 0}\right) \log(0)$$

which is also not defined. Hence, estimation of logistic model is not possible when Pi = 0 and Pi = 1.

In order to avoid above difficulties we consider internal estimation. According to this step technique, we divide individuals into groups. Suppose, there are three types of persons:

N1 = No. of low income persons

N2 = No. of middle income persons.

N3 = No. of high income persons.

Also suppose there are r1 number of person out of n1 persons who makes a choice to purchase a house (scooter) similarly, r2 and r3 out of n2 and n3 respectively who makes a choice of purchase house.

In this case, we assume that:

$$P_i = \frac{ri}{ni}$$

$$\text{i.e. } P_i = \frac{ri}{ni}, P_2 = \frac{r2}{n2}, P_3 = \frac{r3}{n3}$$

In this case, value of Pi lies between the 0 and 1 and hence estimate is possible.

$$\because \quad \log\left[\frac{Pi}{1-Pi}\right] = \log\left[\frac{ri/ni}{1-\frac{ri}{ni}}\right]$$

$$= \log\left[\frac{ri/\not{n}i}{1-\frac{ri}{\not{n}i}}\right]$$

$$= \log\left[\frac{ri}{ni-ri}\right]$$

Above formula is used to determine the values of dependent variables.

Value of xi (income level) are assumed to be given.

So, we can obtain the required data for the estimation of logistic model.

We can use OLs formula technique and find the following logistic model.

$$\log\left[\frac{ri}{ni - ri}\right] = 2 + \hat{B}xi + ei$$

where *ei* regression residual (Greene, 2003 : 675).

Data analysis is presented in the form of Tables, Pie-Charts and Bar Charts etc.

5

Job Satisfaction: A Theoretical Framework

5.1 JOB SATISFACTION

Job satisfaction is the whole matrix of the job factors that make a person like work situation and be willing to go ahead for it without distaste. It comprises of two words "JOB and "SATISFACTION". Job is an occupational activity performed by an individual in return for a reward. Satisfaction refers to the way one feels about events, people, rewards, relations and amount of mental happiness on the job.

It has often been said that a "happy employee is a productive employee" and a happy employee must be satisfied with the job. Since most people spend nearly half of their waking lives at work and the importance of work satisfaction can be well understood. Additionally, job satisfaction usually indicates of results in satisfaction in life in general which is necessary for contentment and happiness. Job satisfaction can be defined as the extent of positive feelings or attitudes that individual have towards their jobs. When a person says that he/she has high job satisfaction, it means that he/she really likes his job, feels good about it and values the job highly and is productive. A satisfied worker is an asset for his organization.

Organisations are concerned with utilizing existing human resources to the optimum level and to make the organization more efficient and effective. It cannot be translated into reality unless and until managerial people will adopt and adapt policies and practices based on the much needed understanding of worker's perception of job satisfaction. Human resources/workers play a vital role in keeping the organization dynamic and vibrant. The extent to which one can give her best to the organization one is working for, depends on the motivation with which one works results in job satisfaction. Job satisfaction is really a great problem in any organizational setting. It is not only faced by industrial workers but also workers (men/women) working in libraries. It, one of the most crucial but controversial issue in behavioral management is very helpful to assess the soundness or health of organization (Garg, 1999, p.109).

The library is the fountain from which the current of culture, enlightenment and new knowledge flows. Though technology has advanced, and electronic gadgets are doing a lot of information processing work in western countries, human resources still plays an overwhelmingly major role in a library. Libraries are labour intensive. And "in a highly labour intensive organization and the major scope for improvement in efficiency and effectiveness must come through more effective use of human resources (Sangam, et al., 1996, p.53-54).

Human resources are the most important and the most costly element of information services. Regardless of the quality of information resources, it would be impossible to speak of proper organization without qualified human resources and motivated personnel.

A library is a dominant agency of dissemination of knowledge. The libraries play a constructive role in the fulfillment of our aspirations and programmes for formal and adult education, Research & Development and industrialization. For successful functioning and performance of its manifold duties, libraries required personnel with a high degree of technical skill, intelligence, imagination, initiative, efficiency and understanding. They are, therefore, not only to be professional qualified, competent and efficient but also to be lively, active, contented and well satisfied with their jobs.

Actually, job satisfaction is generated by individual's perception of how well his/her job on the whole is satisfying to his/her various needs. An individual tries to fulfill his/her variety of needs Job satisfaction refers to the feelings and emotional aspects of individual towards work which is the consequence of the extent of his positive or negative job attitudes (Nandy, 1985, p. 296).

Positive attitude towards the job is conceptually equivalent to job satisfaction. It is only a relative enduring state which undergoes a change with the needs of the individual the capacity of work more situation which fulfills these needs and the individual's own perception of the situation.

This topic (job satisfaction) is receiving increasing academic attention, during the last many years. As a thorough look at the "Library and Information Science Abstracts" shows:

Table 1 : Literature on job satisfaction Noticed in Library and Information Science Abstracts (LISA)

Year	*Number of entries*	*Year*	*Number of entries*
1979	2	1994	4
1980	4	1995	7
1981	2	1996	3
1982	11	1997	2
1983	10	1998	1
1984	1	1999	3
1985	1	2000	4
1986	-	2001	5
1987	-	2002	2
1988	1	2003	3
1989	1	2004	4
1990	4	2005	2
1991	6	2006	4
1992	4	2007	2
1993	5	2008-2012	18

Defining job satisfaction accurately and adequately is no easy task. A review of literature reveals a variety of terms used to describe this phenomenon. However, most analysts agree that job satisfaction is related to the individuals' feeling or emotions towards work rather than to intellectual or rational reactions.

Job satisfaction also lacks satisfactory theory as well as definition about its meaning. The difference in a broad spectrum of views seem to be caused by:

(i) The varied nature of jobs performed by individuals.

(ii) The attempt to conceptualize job satisfaction in a variety of ways by different disciplines like psychology, sociology, education and management.

(iii). The variety of methods employed by various researchers to study job satisfaction.

Job satisfaction is a phenomena that depends on a person's work experience, level of education, ability, personal competence and his identification with the job in question. By the concept of job satisfaction, we understand that perceptions and judgments that depend on the age, education, gender, experience and other personal qualities peculiar to the individual influences job satisfaction (Jordan, 1995, p.23).

Pestonjee (1973, p.58) has suggested that job satisfaction is summation of an employee's feelings in four important areas. Two of them encompass factors directly connected with job (intrinsic factors) and the other two include factors not directly connected with the job but which are presented to have bearing on job satisfaction. These four areas with their related aspects are as follows:

(a) **Job :** Nature of work, hours of work, fellow workers, opportunities on the job, etc.

(b) **Management :** Supervisory treatment, participation, rewards and punishment, praise and blames etc.

(c) **Social relations :** Neighbours, friends and associates, attitude towards people in community etc.

(d) **Personal adjustment :** Emotionality, health, home and living conditions, etc.

The first two together are termed as on-the-job factors while the later two are known as off-the-job factors.

5.2 ON-THE-JOB FACTORS

Pestonjee (1981, p.132) arrived at the following factors related to on-the-job area of satisfaction.

(a) Supervisory treatment/consideration

Important aspects of empathy such as 'sympathetic treatment,' respect for their skill and abilities, opinion seeking, external help to workers, promotion policy, supervisor's behaviour, etc. are included.

(b) Equity regarding work load and pay

As emphasized by numerous investigations, salary is certainly as important factor in job satisfaction. It is one of the fundamental factors in individual's attitude towards his work.

(c) Supportive function

This factor relates to the worker's relations with their supervisor and their interpersonal relations.

(d) Interest in work

If a worker finds his/her work interesting and satisfying, he/she will dissatisfied when deprived of his/her work.

(e) Rules and regulations

It includes over time rules and regulations and discipline.

(f) Intrinsic satisfaction

It includes proper selection of job, nature of work etc. it also includes as to whether the worker considers his/her job respectable and worth doing.

(g) Regard for the organization

This dimension includes the overall management cadre, nature of supervision, and also organisational environment.

(h) Working conditions

It includes tools, material and work equipments, reward for good work and promotion opportunities. Rewards and punishment can be materialistic as well as psychological.

(I) Co-operation of the co-workers

Interactions between members of the group can lead to satisfaction as well as dissatisfaction.

If the work group is believed by an individual to be instrumental to the attainment of positively valent outcomes, it will acquire positive valence for her. If on the other hand, it is perceived to be instrumental to negatively valent outcomes, it will acquire negative valence for her (Vroom, 1964).

(J) Supervision

It includes supervision's attitude towards growth and development of subordinates, as perceived by subordinates.

5.4 OFF-THE-JOB FACTORS

People in an organization are not just a branch of individuals bundled together in a mass. They form groups that are social unities whatever a worker does or feels regarding his/her organization is not only the product of what goes on in the organiastion, rather, his/her attitude and beliefs are affected by factors away from his/her organization or off-the-job factors. Dissatisfaction arising from off-the-job factors are frequently reactions to job conditions. Pestonjee (1981) on the basis of factor analysis brought out eleven factors in off-the-job aspect of job satisfaction:

(a) Relation with family members : It includes interpersonal relations with family members and relatives.

(b) Emotional neuroticism: It includes withdrawal, neurotic anxiety, tiredness etc.

(c) Perception of people in the society: This includes the feelings about society and social bindings.

(d) Anxiety about health: Worry about personal and family health.

(e) Society: The ease with which a person can interact with other people in society and is able to maintain his interpersonal relationship in the society.

(f) Inter Psychic-factors includes : Extroversion, Introversion dimension personality traits. This factor affects the way of working of an individual.

(g) Neighbourhood : Interpersonal relations with surroundings and social ecology.

(h) Interpsychic : It relates with empathy and temperament of the individual.

(i) Trust : It is general indicator of interpersonal trust both in the society and job surroundings.

(j) Isolation : This is indicator of the combined effect of isolation self-estrangement and soul isolation.

(k) Living conditions : It includes workers feelings about environment where he/she lives. It includes home as well as neighbourhood. It may be concluded that it clearly appears that job satisfactions is not only the result of aspects related to work (on-the-job) but is also a product of off-the-job environment.

5.5 DETERMINANTS OF JOB SATISFACTION

There are two variables which determine the job satisfaction: Organisational determinants and personal or Individual determinants.

The level of job determines the job satisfaction. The higher the intensity of job, the greater the satisfaction of individual.

This is because of higher level jobs carry greater prestige and self control. This relationship between occupational level and job satisfaction stems from social reference group theory in that our society values some jobs more than others. Hence, people in valued jobs will like them more than those who are in non-valued jobs. The relationship may also stem from the need fulfillment theory. People in higher level jobs find most of their needs satisfied than people in lower level jobs find their needs unsatisfied.

The different organizational variables which determine job satisfaction of a person are as under:

1. Style of supervision: To a worker, supervision is equally strong contributor to job satisfaction as well as job dissatisfaction. There is positive relationship between the quality of supervision and job satisfaction. The employee-centered supervisory style enhances job satisfaction as he looks after subordinates carefully, displays friendship, respect, dignity and warmth etc. Studies have also indicated that satisfaction tends to be higher when employees believe their supervisor to be competent and takes personal interest in employee's welfare, provides advice and communicates at a personal level. That is why supervision is the most important dimension of quality of working life.

2. Work itself: The nature of work contributes heavily to the feeling of satisfaction. Flexibility, freedom and discretion available in the performance of one's job contributes highly to job satisfaction. Management should introduce a system of job rotation to avoid boredom and to make the work interesting because 'Variety' is the spice of life and man doing the same job for a long time gets fedup and likes change because the nature of job itself is considered as a reason for low work satisfaction.

3. Congenial working environment: In recent years, to manage the diversification of work at work place is an important issue in every organization and working conditions have acquired a special significance in relation to job satisfaction. The work will be more attractive if working environment will be congenial to the task a work proposes to accomplish. Working condition is a broad based concept and includes not only the organizational policies but also the whole work environment. Working conditions should be compatible with an employee's physical comfort. Good working conditions, atmosphere, pleasing surroundings help to increase the production of an organization. Temperature, humidity, ventilation, lighting, hours of work, cleanliness of work place, adequate tools and equipments are the main features which determine job satisfaction.

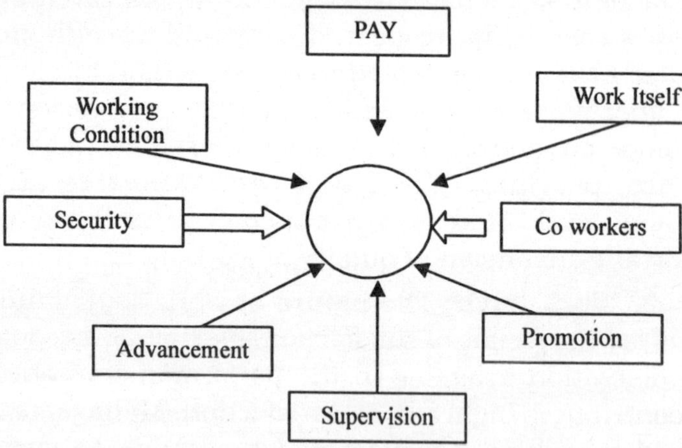

Determinations of Job Satisfaction

4. Pay : To determine job satisfaction, monetary/ financial rewards play a significant role. This is because of two reasons. Firstly, money is an important in fulfillment one's needs and secondly, employees often see pay/salary as a reflection of management is concern and value for them. Employees want a pay system simple, fair and inline with their expectations. Research finds that satisfaction increases when the pay is seen as fair, based on job demands; individual skill level, satisfaction is likely to result.

The importance of pay as a determine in job satisfaction has been greatly over-emphasized by management. It is truthful saying that *"A pay raise is a cure for all which will make everyone in the plant happy."*

5. Promotion : Promotional opportunities determine and affect greatly on job satisfaction. The desire for promotion is generally strong among higher level employees as it involves change in job content, pay, responsibility, independence, social status and the liking. An average employee takes two or three promotions in his entire service and this is the ultimate achievement in his job career and when it is realized, he feels extremely satisfied but when it does not exist, he feels dissatisfied.

6. Co-workers : This aspect determines the degree to which fellow workers are technically proficient and socially supportive. Friendly and cooperative co-workers are a modest source of job satisfaction to individual employee. The work group or work team spirit serves as a source of support, comfort, advice and assistance to the individual worker. On the other hand, if the reverse condition exists, the people are dissatisfied on the work place. This may negative effect on job satisfaction.

7. Job security : since security is a fundamental need, it is more important to the wage one gets or the chances for advancement. It is not sufficient for a man to have his physical needs satisfied. Apart from this, he also wants to ensure that he will continue to be satisfied in future. The man with security feels that he is valued by the institution and that he has the abilities and the opportunities to keep his job regularly. Security is a positive factor which contributes to job satisfaction.

8. Opportunity for advancement : What are the chances of going ahead? This factor ranks high in importance particularly to a person striving for upward mobility. Every young employee whenever he/she joins some organization is full of aspirations. He/she has the drive and desire to go ahead.

5.6 CONCEPTS USED IN THE CONTEXT OF THE PRESENT STUDY

Job Situation

Work environment includes the attitudes and actions of peers, supervisors and the atmosphere they create. It has been concluded in a number of studies that peer groups at work place have definite impact on the performance and job satisfaction of individual. Norms and values pursued by peer groups, attitude of peers, degree of help, guidance and timely support provided by the coworkers and the supervisor have direct bearing on the performance and satisfaction of employees working in the work setting. Reward system, recognition, communication about the policies and practices of organization, respect given by the supervisor for your skill and ability creates job satisfaction. *If rewards go wrong, dissatisfaction arises.* If your supervisor recognizes your good work, appreciates and say a word of two of praise and gives a pat at your back for the good quality of work and you feel yourself satisfied.

On the other hand, in the service oriented organizations, like libraries, both male/female are employed. To serve the libraries efficiently and effectively, mutual adjustment and cooperation by both male/female is necessary to enable women to play their appropriate role without the consideration of sex. Contrary to their traditional attitude towards women, men have to exceed the latter's equality in their relationship with their colleague and sometimes supervise. In order to study the status of women library professionals in libraries, it is also necessary to know about the attitude of males/females superiors, colleagues and the behaviour of subordinates towards them. Hence, different sets of questions have been posed to understand the actual position of women in libraries and specially the attitude of their male counterparts. Hence, the C part of the questionnaire is an attempt to highlight and to surround the working environment or job situation for women librarians.

5.7 JOB MOTIVATION

Currently, there has come about a wide awakening and awareness in India and abroad of the need for increased productivity and this need is gaining momentum with the passage of time.

A potent generator of increased productivity and efficiency in work is adequate motivation of the organisation's human resources.

Rensis Likert, the noted psychologist, while describing motivation, as the core of management has added strength to the common assumption, that "developing a favourable attitude among employees towards the service organizations like libraries will result in increased efficiency and productivity".

"Learn thou, whate'er the motive they may call,
That pleasure is the aim, and self the spring of all"

— ***Robert Sonthey***

Motivation is a general term used to describe the process of starting, directing and maintaining physical and psychological activities. The word 'Motivation' comes from the Latin word *movere* "to move". In a formal sense, motivation is defined as "all those inner striving conditions described as needs, drives, desires, motives and so forth. It is an inner state that activates or moves".

Motivation represents an unsatisfied need which creates a state of tension or disequilibrium, causing the individual to move in a goal directed pattern towards restoring a state of equilibrium by satisfying the need (Singh, 2004, p.119).

According to Beach (1965, p.32) Motivation can be defined, "as a willingness to expand energy to achieve a goal or a reward."

In simple words "Motivation is the strength of drive towards an activity".

In its literal meaning, "Motivation is the act of motivating or providing an incentive".

Motivation is an important part of managing process. Highly qualified and motivated employees are necessary to achieve the objectives of a service organization. It is only through motivation, they contribute maximum to achieve goals. Without motivation, they may not have an urge to maintain or improve their efficiency. Like the other social service institutions, library is also an important service oriented organization that needs the highly motivated and satisfied staff. Motivated librarians help to improve the image of libraries. If employees are motivated, they produce more, they maintain self discipline and productive internal environment in the libraries which ultimately gives better impression to the outsiders dealing with libraries, and its image is enhanced.

5.7.1. Motivation and Job Satisfaction

Every individual has a work to do or a job to perform at work place. Worker's interest and aptitude for a specific job makes his/her placement on the job. Motivation provides more job satisfaction to the employees. Motivation and job satisfaction reinforce each other, strengthen each other and promote each other. Satisfied employee performs better on the job and derives more satisfaction out of it. If the employee is not motivated, his/her level of performance and job satisfaction is low. People join the organizations with certain needs, goals and interests. If the organization fulfills their needs, they get motivated and perform the assigned jobs very efficiently and effectively.

Motivation is a psychological force which is more related with working behaviour of the employees. They can be motivated by providing necessary stimuli by moulding the pattern of behaviour, by providing necessary training for professional growth, supporting facilities etc. To motivate employees, working conditions should be supportive. Cordial relations within the colleagues are most important for motivation. On the other hand, money is also the most important motivator to perform the work properly.

The objective of this section included in the part D of the questionnaire is to assess the extent of motivation with the various factors that result to increase the efficiency in work. These factors include monetary gains, promotional avenues, job security, congenial atmosphere, recognition, self esteem, professional development, and so on. How all these factors are correlated to each other and what is their effect on the performance on job are analysed in the chapter no. 8.

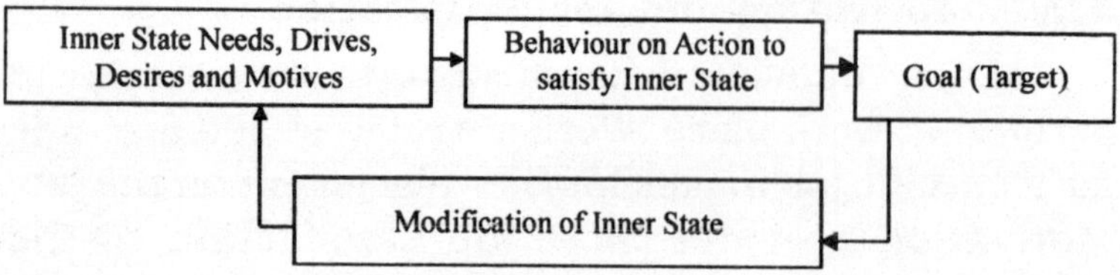

Model of Motivation Process

Source : Human relations and organizational behaviour/ Nirmal Singh, New Delhi : Deep and Deep, 2000 : 73.

5.7.2. Model explained

An unsatisfied need, drive, desire or motive initiates motivation. An unsatisfied need, drive, desire or motive causes tension (Physical, Psychological or sociological) within the individual leading her to engage in some kind of behaviour (to seek a means) to satisfy the need and thereby reduce the tension. This activity is directed towards a goal; arrival at the goal satisfies the need e.g. A thirsty person needs water is driven by thirst and is motivated by a desire for water in order to satisfy the need. Depending on how well the goal is accomplished, the inner stage modified as show by the feedback loop. Thus, motivation begins with an urbanization inner state condition and ends with movement to release that unsatisfied condition, with goal directed behaviour as a part of the process (Zimbardo, 1985, p.263).

5.8 JOB SATISFACTION AND PRODUCTIVITY/ PERFORMANCE

The classic sense of the concept of productivity has been lost today. For more than quantity, productivity now has meaning only to the extent that the goods produced and services rendered are of sufficiently high quality to ensure that the enterprise can successfully complete. That, this in turn requires information technology is undeniable. Productive enterprises are enterprises that are engaged in the contemporary phenomenon of change and development. The more productive and profitable an enterprise is, the more psycho-social security it offers the employee and the more it enhances his/her sense of commitment and belonging.

An employee who makes inadequate use of his/her knowledge and skills in the work place will cause low productivity. Productivity increases in proportion to a worker's utilization of his/her knowledge and skills (Shetty, 1982, p.33). If a person is satisfied with his/her job, he/she will display a positive attitude towards it and his/her desire to succeed in the job will increase accordingly. If this desire is properly channeled by the employer, the result will be an increase in output.

Today the concept and system of total quality management (TQM) is coming to the force in organizations. The human component is being drawn into management and organizations are being re-thought based on this component as a point of departure. Empower people, respect employee's skills and ensure work is interesting and varied. Create a balance between the needs of the organization and take of the individual (Fischer, 1996, p.13).

An effective organizational structure and clear job definition will undoubtedly impact positive on manpower productivity. Similarly, a well-designed work environment, physical structure and economic conditions also have an enhancing effect on manpower productivity. Lawler and Porter, who suggest that productivity creates job satisfaction, have developed models to ensure it in this area (Lawler and Porter, 1968, p.120).

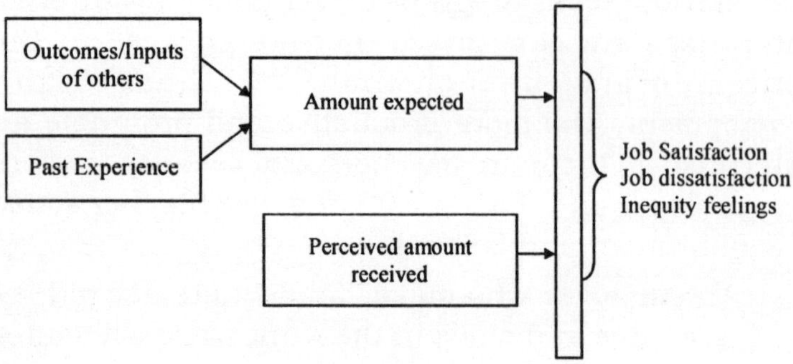

Model of Job Satisfaction

Source: Based on E.E. Lawler III (1973), Motivation in work organizations. Monterey: A: Brooks/Cole: 75.

5.8.1. Model Explained

What determines the level of job satisfaction. The test explanation is provided by the model that combines discrepancy theory and equity theory (Lawler 111, 1973, p.66-69). Discrepancy theory states that the level of job satisfaction is determined by the discrepancy between what people expect to receive and what they experience (McFarlin and Rice, 1992, p.46). Equity theory is a motivational theory that explains how people develop perceptions of fairness in the distribution and exchange of resources. This theory occurs when the person and comparison with other have similar outcome/input ratio. This is relevant to job satisfaction because the amount we expect to receive is partly determined by our comparison with other people.

In summary, discrepancy and equity theories predict that as reality meets and exceeds expectations, job satisfaction will increase. Job satisfaction begins to decrease when the perceived job situation is so much better than expected that the over-reward creates a feeling of guilt or unfairness.

5.9 RECRUITMENT AND PROMOTION POLICY

Recruitment is a process of reaching for prospective employees and stimulating and encouraging them to apply for job in an organization. It involves commitment by the employer to find and employ the best qualified persons, to retain the best and most promising of those hired and to provide programmes and facilities for personnel growth on the job.

People in an organization determine the performance capacity of the organization. People are truly the most precious resource of any organization. Therefore, increasing attention is being of an individual worker and or working groups for their efficient and effectivc use to achieve organizational goals.

The opportunity for advancement is regarded fundamental. Hence, promotion programmes are provided in organizations and professions as career systems for vertical movement. A promotion is reassignment of the individual to a job of higher rank. In our society, promotions are much coveted to satisfy individual aspirations to reach higher positions or advancement. They bring higher status, more authority, less close supervision, greater freedom. Usually, promotion accompanies better grades pay and perks and better standard and living.

Promotion is one of the factors which motivates employees to work efficiently in an organization. It refers to the onward movement of an employees to work efficiently in an organization. It refers to the upward movement of an employee in the job hierarchy. It involves changes in rewards, co-workers, responsibility, supervision and the task itself. Opportunity for promotion is known to have a vital influence on job satisfaction of the employees. This is very essential for women employees who are very few in number and almost those women are dissatisfied who have no climbed up the promotion ladder during their service period.

This part of the present study attempts to highlight some variables shown in the E part of the questionnaire by asking questions from the women respondents regarding recruitment and promotion policy in libraries. How these variables are correlated to each other and how they affect job satisfaction are evaluated in the chapter no. 8.

5.10 JOB AND FAMILY

Family is the area in which the role of women is traditionally the most prominent. Any change in their position reflects in their activities within the family and it also affect all the family members. So, the family provides the most suitable area for examining the change in women's status brought about by their employment. The employed women holds an advantageous position in family due to their employment.

It is a generally accepted fact that the participation of women in employment outside home has greatly changed their family lives. Perhaps. The most far-reaching effect has been the economic independence attained by working women. Another possible effect is the redistribution of the work within the family so that the employed women can still participation in their work while continuing many of their traditional familial obligations. Tasks assigned to the wife are being assumed or shared by the husband and other family members jointly so that the wife can have near equal responsibility for earning the family living. The salary income of a working women is a substantial contribution to the family income which could be expected to give her greater interests in financial decisions and greater respects from her husband and other family members. Her job provides her a chance to make contacts with fellow workers which lessens her dependence on her husband for emotional support and increases the skill and knowledge she brings to decision making. Such factors make them resourceful and competent decision-makers. Participation of women in the work outside the home has tended to minimize the restricted behaviour of husband.

Work situation will always have a bearing upon the work participants. Employment may foster in them a dynamic and pragmatic approach to life, an individualistic view of life and also a cosmopolitan orientation towards life. There is every possibility that these attitudes are reflected in the working women's pattern of family life.

In order to assess the status of women library professionals in the family as a result of employment; the variables which are important determinants of status within the family and how these variables are correlated to each other are analysed in chapter no. 8.

5.11 PERSONAL LIFE SATISFACTION

Work forms an important part of our life. The occupational role of women enables them to have a wider perspective on life. It provides opportunities for making acquaintances' with a wide variety of people and for participating actively in the larger social life. It also exposes them to new situations and experiences which results in a more balanced development of their personality. An employed women has greater freedom in family decision making, greater latitude in spending family income and more equal opportunity in interpersonal relationship within the family and lesser burden of work at home. Decision making in the family is a critical element in the status of family members since it involves the allocation of resources and the distribution of sales within the family. Economic independence is also chosen because the wife also contributes to the family income.

So, the employment of women contributes some changes in the traditional norms and an increase in women's power in the family and their status. Her contribution to the family income enables her to have a voice in the spending of income and greater cooperation and respect from other family members. Economic and social independence provides satisfaction.

Satisfaction with children is very important especially when they are grown ups. If they disobey their parents or misbehave, this will have a reflection on the women's satisfaction on job. Attitude of husband and the other family members also contributes women's satisfaction on the job. If the husband and her in-laws expect her to perform all the traditional and regular domestic activities, perhaps she fails to perform all these responsibilities. Overburden of work leads to frustration which causes dissatisfaction on the job. Worry about her own health and family health creates dissatisfaction. Sometimes, their neighbourer creates problems due to jealous nature because of her job that creates dissatisfaction for working women. Various studies have been conducted to find the relationship between life satisfaction which includes personal and social factors and job satisfaction.

While the external environment within the organization and the nature of the job are important determinants of job satisfaction, personal attributes of individual employees play a very important role as to whether they are happy at the job or not. People with generally negative attitudes about life and pessimists always complaint about everything including the job. No matter how good the job is, such people always find something wrong with it to complain about.

Age, seniority and tenure have considerable influence on job satisfaction. It is expected that as people grow older, they usually come up the corporate ladder with the passage of time and move into more challenging and responsible positions. Meeting these challengs and succeeding is a high source of satisfaction. Even if they donot move up in their position, it is equally natural to assume that with age, people become more mature and realistic and less idealistic so that they are willing to accept available resources and rewards and be satisfied about the situation. Employees who do not move up at all with time are more likely to be dissatisfied with their jobs.

Equally important is the intrinsic source of satisfaction which comes from the person and is a function of the employee's personality. Some of the personality traits that are directly related to increase job satisfaction are self assurance, self esteem, maturity, decisiveness, sense of autonomy, challenge and responsibility. It can be concluded that the higher the person is in Maslow's model of hierarchical needs, the higher is the job satisfaction (Singh, 2004, p.164).

So, the conditions of work and life of a person can be responsible for the job dissatisfaction. Therefore, an attempt to find out the perceptions of women librarians about society, social bindings and the factors affecting their personal life and job satisfaction.

6

Demographic Profile of Women Library Professionals

In order to assess the information about job satisfaction among the women library professionals, printed copies of questionnaires were distributed to respondents to fill in. In last part of the questionnaire, the respondents were asked to provide general information about themselves.

This chapter provides general information about their Age, Marital status, Occupational status of husband, Family background, Nature of family, Academic qualification, Professional qualification, Improvement in qualification, Experience in job, Promotion in job, Designation and pay scale etc.

At the last, some another affecting factors/ variables related to job have also being studied in this chapter.

The motive to collect information about respondents has a great bearing on their job, their working and behaviour.

Table 1 : Age group of the women library professionals

S. No.	Age group (in years)	No. of Women library professionals =200 Number	%age
1.	21 – 30	47	23.5
2.	31 – 40	26	13.0
3.	41 – 50	74	37.0
4.	51 +	53	26.5
	Total	200	100

It has been revealed in Table – 1 that the percentage 37.0 percent age of women respondents in the age group of 41-50, is quite higher than other who are in the age group of 51 + who are 26.5 percent. Women under age group of 21 -30 is 23.15 percent and under age group of 31 – 40 is 13.0 percent.

Table 2 : Marital Status of Women Library Professionals

S. No.	Marital Status	No. of Women library professionals =200 Number	%age
1.	Married	172	86
2.	Unmarried	28	14
	Total	200	100

It is clear from Table 2 that overwhelming majority of respondents 86 percent are married and 14 percent are unmarried. The reason for such difference is that in the recent years more of young females are entering the library profession. Now the profession has become female oriented.

It is clear from Table – 1 of age that the percentage of respondents in the age group of 21 – 30 years is right age for the marriage according to our culture. It may be mentioned here that only a negligible percentage of women are divorced or under another marital complication.

Table 3 : Occupational Status of Women Librarian's Husband (Total Married = 172)

S. No.	*Occupational status*	*No. of Women library professionals =200*	
		Number	*%age*
1.	Govt. Job	86	43
2.	Pvt. Job	42	21
3.	Agriculturist and others	44	22
	Total	172	86

Table 3 revealed the data that 43 percent of the respondent's husbands are serving on government jobs as A class and B class employees. The persons occupying the job in private sector are 21 percent. The respondents belonging to rural family background, the occupation of their husbands is agriculture i.e. 22 percent. It is clear from the above information that majority of the persons are in government jobs. It can be estimated that double earning people are satisfied comparatively to others.

Table 4 : Family Background of Women Library Professionals

S. No.	*Family Background*	*No. of Women library professionals =200*	
		Number	*%age*
1.	Urban	154	77
2.	Rural	46	23
	Total	200	100

Table 4 indicates that overwhelming majority of the respondents i.e 77 percent belong to urban areas. Only 23 percent thereof belong to rural areas. As per information ascertained even respondents born in rural areas were also settled and working in urban areas.

Table 5 : Nature of family of women library professionals

S. No.	*Nature of Family*	*No. of Women library professionals =200*	
		Number	*%age*
1.	Joint	47	23.5
2.	Nuclear	153	76.5
	Total	200	100

Table 5 revealed that overwhelming majority of respondents belong to nuclear families, i.e. 76.5 percent and 23.5 percent belong to joint families. There is much difference found for family aspect.

Table 6 : Number of Dependents of Women Library Professionals including Children and Others

S. No.	*Number of Dependants*	*No. of Women library professionals =200*	
		Number	*%age*
1.	Three	132	66
2.	More than three	68	34
	Total	200	100

Table 6 showed that the overwhelming majority of the respondents i.e. 66 percent have maximum three dependants including their children and other family members and mostly belong to urban areas. 34 percent have within four to five dependents. Among them, some respondents belong to joint families and have double responsibility to look after their children and in-laws. It can be observed that the respondents with double burden remain less satisfied in comparison to others who live in nuclear families with less dependents.

Table 7 : Academic Qualification of Women Library Professionals

S. No.	Academic Qualification	No. of Women library professionals =200 Number	%age
1.	Graduates	62	31
2.	Post-Gradates	130	65
3.	Ph.D. in Humanities / Social Sciences	8	4
	Total	200	100

Breakup of the respondents according to their academic qualification is given in Table 7. Majority i.e 65 percent of the respondents are post-graduates. A negligible percentage of respondents was found to be double post-graduates i.e. 3 percent. Respondents possessing doctoral degree in different faculties are 4 percent.

Table 8 : Professional Qualifications of Women Library Professionals

S. No.	Professional Qualification	No. of Women library professionals =200 Number	%age
1.	B. Lib. Sc.	66	33
2.	M. Lib. Sc.	134	67
	Total	200	100

A detailed information about the professional qualifications of the respondents is given in Table 8. It is evident from the table that most of the university and college librarians possess master's degree in Library Science; M.Lib. Sc. i.e. 67 percent. It is very interesting to note and mention here that 8 percent women librarians have gained doctoral degrees in library science and 4 percent are in pipeline as they are about to complete their doctorate degrees in the same field.

Young women are better qualified than others as it should be because to cope with rising and demanding services and the changing environment of the libraries.

Table 9 : Factors responsible for the improvement in qualification (Academic and Professional) by women library professionals

S. No.	*Improvement in Qualification (Academic/ Professional)*	*No. of Women library professionals =200*	
		Number	*%age*
1.	Administrative requirements	99	49.5
2.	Personal/famillial requirements	76	38
3.	No improvement	25	12.5
	Total	200	100

Table 10 : Professional Experience of Women Library Processional

S. No.	*Professional Experience*	*No. of Women library professionals =200*	
		Number	*%age*
1.	< 5	22	11.0
2.	6 – 10	31	15.5
3.	11 – 20	65	32.5
4.	21>	82	41.0
	Total	200	100

Table 10 is for respondents distribution according to experience (professional) in the present job. The percentage of respondents having professional experience of 5 year or less than 5 years is only 11.0 percent while having experience of 6 – 10 is 15.5 percent. This manifests that more of women have joined this profession during the recent years. 41.0 percent of the respondents are in the category of having professional experience of 21 years or more. Respondents having professional experience between 11 – 20 years is 32.5 percent. This table indicates that women are entering this profession speedily. On the other hand, it shows that experience depends on duration or tenure of work on job.

Table 11 : Women Library Professionals having Promotion

S. No.	*Promotion During Job*	*No. of Women library professionals =200*	
		Number	*%age*
1.	Women with promotion	88	44%
2.	Women without promotion	112	56%
	Total	200	100%

This table revealed that 44 percent women got promoted during their job and it is very interesting to note that among them 12 percent got promotion twice during their job. The number of women with single promotion is 32 percent. The reason behind the promotion may be personal pulls or impartiality etc. as stated by the unpromoted women.

56 percent women got not even a single promotion during their job despite of well qualified and having professional experience of more than 16-18 years. It is a very distressing factor in this profession.

All the respondents were categorized according to their designations and pay scales which has been shown in Table 12. The data revealed that only 1 percent of the total respondents are working in the pay scale of Rs. 37,400-67,000as university Librarian. The percentage of women respondents working as Dy.

Table 12 : Designation and Pay Scale of Women Library Professionals

S. No	Designation	Pay Scale (Revised) Rs.	No. of Women library professionals =200 Number	%age
1.	University Librarian	37,400-67,000 AGP 10,000	2	1
2.	Dy. Librarian in University/Selection Grade Librarian in College	15,600-39,100 AGP 8,000	16	8
3.	Asstt. Librarian in University Sr. Scale/Senior Librarian in College	15,600-39,100 AGP 7,000	29	14.5
4.	Asstt. Librarian in University/Librarian in College	15,600-39,100 AGP 6,000	54	27
5.	Library Asstt./ Professional Asstt. In University/ Asstt. Librarian in College.	10,300-34,800 AGP 3800	43	21.5
6.	Library Restorers in University/Library Asstt. in college	5910-20,300 AGP 2000	56	28

Librarian in the university/selection grade librarian in colleges in the pay scale of Rs. 15,600-39,100 is 8 percent. A total of 14.5 percent respondents are in the group of Asstt. Librarian in university, Sr. Scale/senior librarian in colleges in the pay scale of Rs. 15,600-39,100. Out of 200 respondents, 54 are in the group i.e. 27 percent who are working as Asstt. Librarian in university/librarian in college in the pay scale of 15,600-39,100.

Total 21.5 percent are designated as Library Assistants / Professional Assistants. In universities,

Assistants librarians in colleges are working in the pay scale of 10,300-34,800. 28 percent are working as Library Restorers in university/Library Assistants in colleges are working in the pay scale of 5,910-20,300. Majority of the women respondents i.e. 50.5 percent working on the higher ranks while 49.5 percent are on Junior posts.

Table 13 : Personal perceptions of the factors by Women Library Professionals = 200

S. No.	*Factors*	*Yes*	*No*
1.	Any training in computer applications	49%	51%
2.	Perception about computerization of libraries	48.5%	51.5%
3.	Published work	28%	72%
4.	Attend seminars, conferences, refresher courses etc. for professional development	36%	64%
5.	Duty leave, financial assistance to attend the professional activities	19%	81%
6.	Membership of any professional association	26.5%	73.5%
7.	Satisfaction with the working of association for library profession	18%	82%

200 women library professionals were asked some questions regarding their personal views and professional achievements to know the effect of these factors on their job satisfaction.

It may be noted that, only 28 percent librarians have some published work while 64 percent of the respondents have never attended any conference and seminar and 81 percent of them have never availed any duty leave or financial assistance to participate in academic professional activities for their continued education and professional development. Professional awareness is not very high as 73.5 percent are not even member of any professional association.

Membership of a professional association is very motivating factor for job satisfaction. Low membership of associations may be due to the reason that people are not happy with the working and efforts of the library associations for the librarians.

Computers play an important role in library services and management. But regretfully more than half i.e. 51 percent have no training in computers and accordingly so much percentage of the respondents do not find any use in computerization of the library work and services.

So, these views cannot be supported by the new demands of the users. Such persons cannot perform any useful work in the libraries and consequently will have no job satisfaction.

7

Factors in Job Satisfaction of Women : A Case of Librarians

"Lack of job satisfaction kills professionalism"

— Ramesh and Raju, 2002, p. 126

An analysis of job satisfaction within an organization provides an important diagnostic assessment of the health of the organization. Employee's reactions to organizational structure, job environment, personell policies, professional milieu, social environment, working conditions and other organizational characteristics are one form of feedback to the administration pertaining to its performance (D' Elia, 1979, p.283)

Generally, two approaches have been adopted in the study of job satisfaction. It has been measured as either unidimensional or a multidimensional approach that a worker tends to think of his/her as a whole. The multidimensional view of job satisfaction as the worker's attitude to many aspect of the job. (Nazoota, 1985, p. 77) This study also analysed different aspect of job satisfaction.

Analysis of data has been divided into following parts:

The beginning part of this chapter throws light on women's perceptions about library profession and their original motivation, expectations and satisfaction from it.

The next part of this chapter reveals all the factors associated with job satisfaction in the context of present study and the ranks given by the respondents for their satisfaction level to every factor.

Corelational analysis of data is presented in the last part of this chapter.

7.1. LIBRARY PROFESSION: AN ANALYSIS

Librarians are important part of the society since ancient times. For the last century, librarianship and information services have grown into a multidisciplinary profession. In the information society, the value of library services has increased many times and the profession has grown into many directions touching many fields from philosophy to computers and from sociology to economics. The profession has grown technologically and strengthwise. Its importance for economical, educational and technological growth of a society cannot be denied. Library and information services are required in every field of society. Due to its growth, many research studies have been done to improve its services, functioning and image. Since human resources are very important part of any profession. Therefore, many studies regarding manpower development, library education, their work environment, their social and psychological problems have been done. Women have been very sizeable part of the work force in libraries and they have their own problems different from their male counterparts.

Therefore, the objective of this section included in the questionnaire is to assess some personal characteristics of library profession pertaining to females which concerns the original motivation towards librarianship.

Original motivation towards librarianship includes the statements given in Table No.1.

Table 1 : Factors showing original motivation for Library Profession

1.	Why did you opt for Library Profession?		
	By Choice		73 %
	Due to circumstances		23 %
	Any other reason		4 %
2.	When did you decide to join the profession?		
	While purusing studies In School/College/ University		33.5 %
	After the School/ College/University education		60.5 %
	While in service		6 %
3.	What motivated you most to join this profession?		
	3.1	Better job prospects	31%
	3.2	Equality with academic staff in respect of status	14%
	3.3	Job attraction	27%
	3.4	Good salary	9.5%
	3.5	No other alternative available	16.5%
	3.6	Any other reason	2%
4.	Who motivated you to join this profession?		
	4.1	Parents	48.6%
	4.2	Friends	23.5%
	4.3	Teachers	8.2%
	4.4	Librarians	12%
	4.5	Any other	7.7%

The highest percentage is scored by those who claim to have opted the profession by choice because they i.e. 73 percent are positively attracted to it. 23 percent respondents came towards it due to circumstances. Remaining 4 percent refused to answer this question.

Majority of respondents i.e. 60.5 percent decided to join librarianship after the completion of their academic qualification. 33.5 percent thought about it during their study. Remaining 6 percent women came towards it when they were engaged in some other private job.

When asked what attracted them more to the profession, majority of the respondents i.e. 31 percent said that it was job prospects. Job attraction came second in rank i.e. 27 percent while unfortunately 16 percent people came to the profession only for employment as there was no other job for them. About 10 percent people motivated to the profession due to good salary. Most of the new entrants 7.7 percent have no idea about the nature and value of library profession. They are encouraged and guided by many people in their contacts. In our study, most of the female entrants i.e. 48.6 percent were guided by their parents. They were followed by friends 23.5 percent and the librarians came at number 12 percent as motivator. Some about 8.2 percent were motivated by their teachers.

Regarding their rethinking, 81.6 percent of the respondents were happy over the choice of their profession but unfortunately, 18.4 percent thought they made a mistake in joining this profession. It means that majority of the respondents are happy and satisfied.

Out of 200 respondents, 27.6 percent thought of joining many other professions before joining this profession namely banking, teaching, nursing, social welfare, marketing etc.

Table 2

S. No.	*Factors showing right choice of librarianship*	*Yes*	*No*
1.	Do you think that you have selected the right profession for you?	81.6%	18.4%
2.	Did you think of joining any other profession/s also before joining this profession	27.6%	72.4%
3.	Idea to change the profession with the same monetary gains	42.5%	57.5%
4.	Would you recommend to others your profession for early employment	50%	50%
5.	Respectable profession	78.8%	21.2%
6.	If you start your career all over again, will you like to join this profession again?	61.4%	38.6%

Significant majority of respondents i.e. 57.5 percent revealed that they are not willing to change their present profession with the same monetary perks/ gains.

It is very healthy and quite satisfactory aspect for the profession. Out of the total number 42.5 percent are willing to change this profession because of many reasons.

Half of the total respondents i.e. 50 percent have no hesitation to recommend the library profession to others as a place of early employment but 50 percent have negative thinking because their own family members are wandering here and there for a long time to seek a appropriate job with adequate salary even after getting post graduation in library science. Moreover, jobs are neither lucrative nor attractive otherwise.

Regarding the status of the profession in the eyes of others, about 80 percent thought this profession is respectable and they get due respect while 20 percent don't think so. Majority of the respondents i.e. 61.4 percent are very much interested in this profession. They stated that they joined librarianship by choice. But 38.6 percent answered in negative due to many reasons such as stagnation in promotion even after having good academic record as well as professional record, unsatisfactory working conditions, low salary and non cooperation within the family library staff. It reveals that they are totally dissatisfied. They will never like to adopt this profession in case they get choice to start their career again.

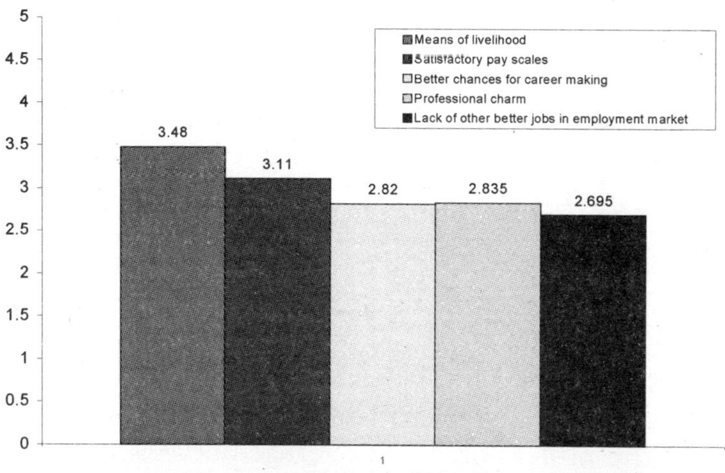

Factors showing the ranks for motivation to stick to "Library Profession"

Part A of the questionnaire
Q No. (11)

In library profession, the mean value for factors that stick the women librarians most to this profession has been calculated and the result shows that means of livelihood and satisfactory pay scales get highest ranks respectively as compared to other factors. The professional charm, better chances for career making and lack of other better jobs in market respectively get least ranks.

Now let's examinc the community wise ranking of the status of the profession. The frequency distribution for the three types of communities: Academic community, Public community and Family community, have been given in the following Table-3 along with the ranking of type in parenthesis.

Table 3 : How do the Academic Community, Public and Your Family Rank the Status of Library Profession?

Community'→ Sr. No.	*Preference*	*Academic Number of Persons*	*Public Number of Persons*	*Family Number of Persons*
1	Very High	23 (4)	20 (4)	72 (1)
2	High	55 (2)	66 (2)	61 (2)
3	Average	83 (1)	80 (1)	39 (3)
4	Low	32 (3)	25 (3)	15 (4)
5	Very Low	07 (5)	09 (5)	13 (5)

Author's Calculations

It is evident from above Table 3 that most of the persons belonging to academic and public community rank the profession as an average one. On the other hand from the hindsight of a family members, the profession secures the very high dignity. The frequency distributions have been given in the diagrams 1, 2 and 3 for the academic, public and family community.

It is evident from figures 1 and 2, that the distribution is approximately same. The characteristics of both of the series do not differ significantly. Hence, we can say that the academic and public community's choice about the profession is same. But choice the third class's i.e. the choice of family community is different. The family community ranks the status of the profession very high. This sample's characteristics are entirely and statistically different from the other two samples.

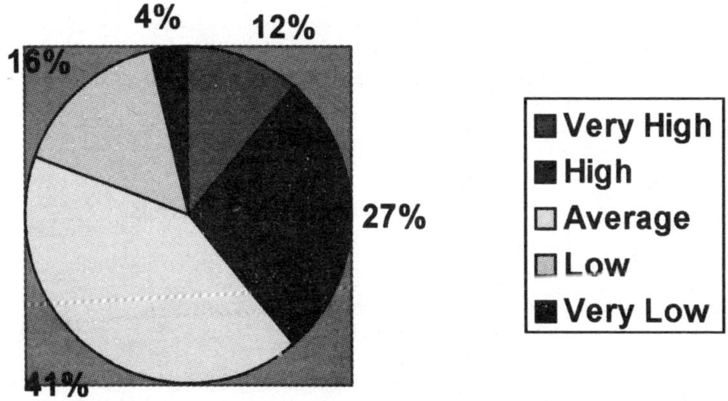

Fig. 1 : Pie Chart for the Distribution of Number of Persons Ranking the Status of Library Profession

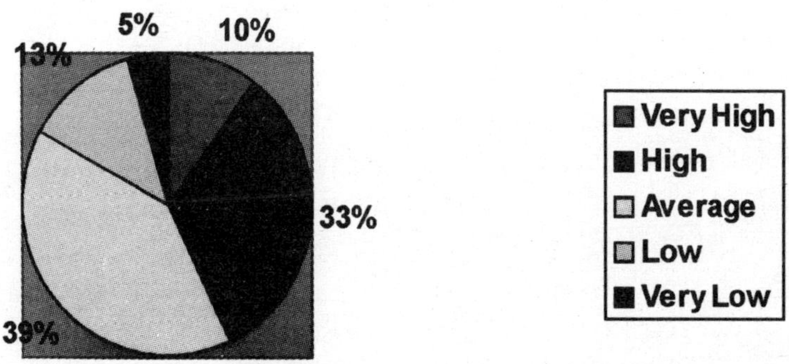

Fig. 2 : Pie Chart for the Distribution of Number of Persons Ranking the Status of Library Profession

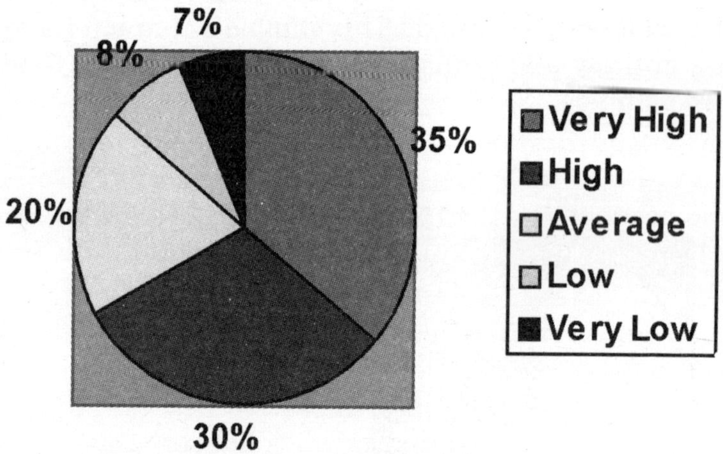

Fig. 3 : Pie Chart for the Distribution of Number of Persons Ranking the Status of Library Profession

7.2 JOB SATISFACTION OF WOMEN LIBRARIANS IN THE CONTEXT OF PRESENT STUDY:

The objective of this section under the title job satisfaction (part B of the questionnaire) is to assess the job satisfaction of women librarians with respect to on-the-job and off-the-job factors affecting job satisfaction. These factors are assessed by percentage distribution. Statements are given in the Table 4 and Table 5. On-the-job factors include job and management, Off-the-job factors include personal adjustment and social relations.

In this section 44 variables (32 on-the-job and 12 off-the-job) were formulated to measure the job satisfaction level of female workers in the libraries. These on-the-job factors varied from nature of job, salary and perks, work load and relation with colleagues and off-the-job factors are mostly concerned with personal and family life. 87 percent of respondents rated job security on number one. It may be noted that under the job security act even the employees working in affiliated and aided colleges, are covered by the job security act. Judicial courts and labour courts are always particular about the security of workers. So the management and the employees do not terminate the services of the employees without proper, concrete and serious reasons. Hence, this factor did not matter much with the confirmed employees. But it will matter in the days when the people are hired on contract basis.

Table 4 : On-the-job factors include job and management showing satisfaction/ dissatisfaction level

Sr. No.	*Factors/ Variables*	*Satisfied*	*Dissatisfied*
1.	Nature of Job		
	1.1 Routine	34 %	
	1.2 Challenging	11.0 %	
	1.3 Boring	5.5 %	
	1.4 Interesting	49.0 %	
2.	Variation of Job	74.7 %	25.3%
3.	Cooperation from the supervisor	80 %	20%
4.	Independence	66.3 %	33.7%
5.	Suitable working hours	61 %	39%
6.	Salary	69%	31%
7.	Fringe benefits	75%	25%
8.	Supporting facilities	70.6%	27.4%
9.	Job security	87%	13%
10.	Impartiality	60%	40%
11.	Supervisor's attitude	73.1%	26.9%
12.	Incentives and recognition	30 %	70%
13.	Staff strength	40 %	60%
14.	Coordination among staff members	34.6 %	65.4%
15.	Treatment of Authorities	50.5 %	49.5%

16.	In-Service training for professional development	29.6 %	70.4%
17.	Lack of time for taking higher responsibilities	44.9 %	55.1%
18.	Satisfactory promotional avenues	44 %	56%
19.	Satisfactory recruitment and promotion policy	52.6 %	47.4%
20.	Good chances for promotion	39.4 %	60.6%
21.	Justice and honesty observed in giving promotion	30 %	70%
22.	Service/working conditions	55.1%	44.9%
23.	Individually identity	25%	75%
24.	Respectable job according to your skill & personality	16%	84%
25.	Work Load	44%	56%
26.	Difficulty to take leave	32%	68%
27.	Tiredness	31%	68%
28.	Tension/Anxiety	32%	68%
29.	Work with unpleasant people	53.5%	46.5%
30.	Hurt with small incidents on-the-job	44.8%	55.2%
31.	Satisfactory rules to secure female staff	68.8%	31.2%
32.	Improvement in the living standard due to this job	63%	37%

The second highly valued parameter is cooperation from the supervisor. 80percent have mentioned that they get cooperation from the supervisor. It is very important for job productivity and satisfaction. I think that rest of the 20 percent who are not having cooperation may be due to personal reasons. Job variation has been ranked at 3rd position with 75 percent. It is very positive approach because workers learnt different jobs and have exposure for different skills. It develops confidence and better understanding of the institutional work. It also saves employees from boredom and burnout. The other factor having the same rank i.e 3rd is fringe benefits. It is also very important that more than the regular salary, fringe benefits and perks should be increased.

The other factors to which the respondents have values are supervisor's attitude 73.1 percent, supporting facilities 70.6 percent, salary 69 percent and the physical security of female staff 68.8 percent.

The factors which have got middle ranks are independence 66.3 percent, impartiality 60 percent, working conditions 55.1 percent, work load 44 percent, hurt with small incidents on-the-job 44.8 percent. The factors which are least preferred are incentive and recognition 30 percent, lack of promotion avenues 44 percent, individual identity 25 percent and justice in giving promotions 30 percent and lack of professional development 70.4 percent. These are the most important factors which create job satisfaction but it is very distressing that female workers showed their dissatisfaction with these factors.

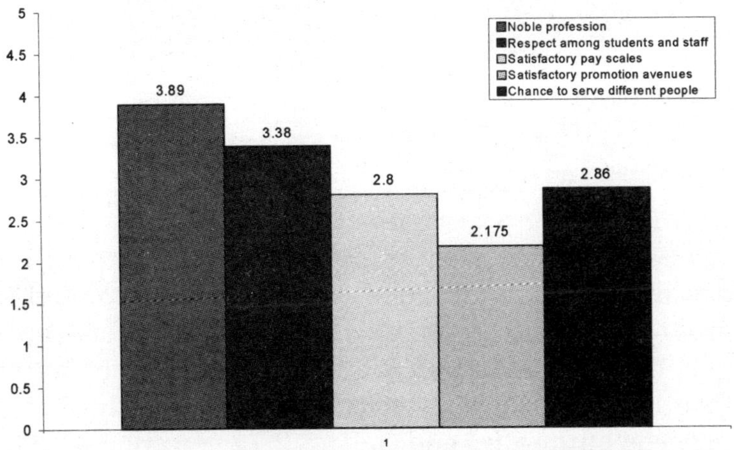

Factors showing the ranks for job satisfaction
Part B of the questionnaire
Q No. (9)

The mean values of job satisfaction taking into account five factors like noble profession, respect among students and staff pay scales promotion avenues and chance to serve different people have been calculated. The factor noble profession gets highest rank and satisfactory promotion avenues get the least rank.

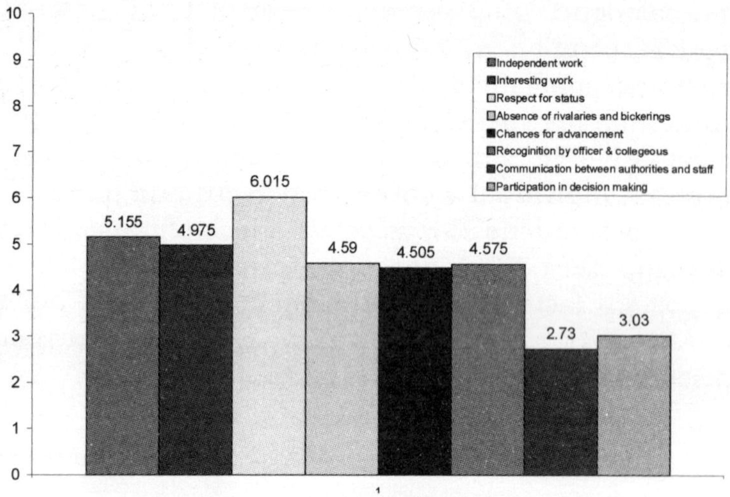

Factors showing ranks for the most important conditions of job satisfaction Part B of the questionnaire Q No. (6)

The mean values for the most important conditions of job satisfaction have been calculated in order of ranks priority. The factors respect for status gets the highest rank i.e. 6.015 percent as compared to other conditions and the factor communication between authorities and staff i.e. 2.73 percent gets least priority for job satisfaction.

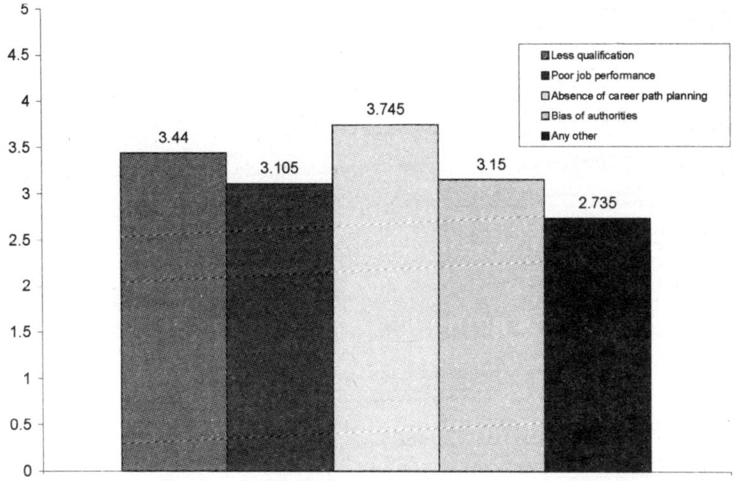

Factors showing the ranks for stagnation in promotion
Part E of the questionnaire
Q No. (5)

In recruitment and promotion policy, the mean values of ranks for stagnation in present position of women librarians has been calculated. Are the women library professionals satisfied or not with promotion policy. In such case, absence of the career path planning gets highest priority i.e. 3.745 percent as compared to others. Like less qualification, poor job performance, bias of authorities and any other etc.

Regarding off-the-job factors, the highly ranked factor is pleasantly passing time at home i.e 91.2 percent. Congenial atmosphere at home creates full satisfaction at job. Then the other equally ranked factors are improvement in qualification i.e. 86.5 percent. Economic independence 85.6 percent leads the power for decision making 83 percent at home. And the next factor showed satisfaction is neighbourhoo. But the factors that showed dissatisfaction are caste discrimination in the society and worry about family health and her own health also. The highly dissatisfied factor ranked 85.3 percent i.e. non-cooperation from family members. And it is a very negative finding which effects seriously on-the-job productivity and satisfaction of female workers because female employees give no fruitful results to the institution without the cooperation from the family and colleagues on-the-job.

Table 5 : Off-the-job factors include personal adjustment and social relations showing satisfaction/ dissatisfaction level

Sr. No.	Factors/ Variables	Satisfied	Dissatisfied
1.	Pleasantly pass your time at home	91.2%	8.8%
2.	Cooperation from family members	14.7%	85.3%
3.	Capable to deal with family responsibility with job	67%	33%
4.	Worry about family health	21.9%	78.1%
5.	Respect given by family	76%	24%
6.	Improvement of qualification to raise the standard of living	86.5%	13.5%
7.	Economic independence due to job	85.6%	14.4%
8.	Decision making power at home	83%	17%
9.	Empowerment to deal with social traditions	75.3%	24.7%
10.	Caste discriminations	28.4%	71.6%
11.	Your own health makes you mentally disturb	26.3%	73.7%
12.	Neighbourhood	78.9%	21.1%

How these factors are correlated to and affected by each other are analysed in the last part of this chapter no. 8.

7.3 CORRELATIONAL ANALYSIS OF DATA

The present part of this chapter is an attempt to determine the major on-the-job and off the-job factors, determining the job satisfaction among the women library professionals working in the libraries. The analysis is carried out using the different statistical techniques based upon multivariate regression analysis and correlation analysis. The entire part of this chapter has been distributed among six different sections. In section- I, the empirical substantiation based upon the co-relational analysis has been presented. Section- II deals with the factors affecting job satisfaction determined using the stepwise regression technique. In section- III, an alternative technique of factor analysis has been applied to determine the factors affecting job satisfaction, dissatisfaction and job situation. Section-IV deals with the on-the-job and off-the-job factors affecting job satisfaction. The section-V presents the evidence pertaining to the demographic factors affecting job satisfaction. The Logistic Model has been applied here because of the qualitative nature of the dependent variable. The last section-VI presents the major conclusions derived from this part.

SECTION-I : CO-RELATIONAL ANALYSIS

The product moment Karl Pearson's Coefficient of Correlation method has been used in this section to analyze.

(i) Inter-correlation among the factors what make the job satisfying for a person;

(ii) Inter-correlation among the behavioural components of the supervisor to provide job satisfaction;

(iii) Inter-correlation among the motivational factors for increasing efficiency of work;

(iv) Inter-correlation among the recruitment and promotion policy variates;

(v) Inter-correlation among the job and family independence;

(vi) Inter-correlation among the personal and social factors.

(i) Inter-correlation among the factors what make the job satisfactory for a Worker

Table-I represents the correlational analysis showing the inter-correlational among the factors what make the job satisfactory for a person. As $r_{12} = r_{21}$, therefore the matrix is symmetric one and hence we have not filled the upper diagonal triangle.

In the Table I, nobility of the profession is negatively related with the other four factors and the coefficients are significant at 99 percent confidence level except the fourth variable i.e. chance to serve different people. This variable is also negatively related with nobility of profession but the relationship is insignificant and can be ignored.

Respect among the students and staff is also negatively related with the remaining four factors. The affect of nobility of profession, satisfactory pay scales and satisfactory promotion avenues is significant at 0.01 level of significance. But the relationship of respect among students and staff and chance to serve different peoplc is insignificant at both 0.01 and 0.05 level of significance.

Due to positive theoretical relationship between promotion and pay scales, the third variable satisfactory pay scales has positive correlation with the satisfactory promotion avenues but this coefficient is insignificant statistically. All other three variables are negatively and significantly related with the satisfactory pay scales.

The fourth variable of Table-I is negatively related with all other variables except the satisfactory pay scales. Remaining three variables are affecting significantly with the negative coefficient.

Table 6 : Correlation Matrix of 5×5 showing inter-correlation among the factors what makes the job satisfactory for a person

S. No.	Variable	1	2	3	4	5
1	Nobility of profession	1.000				
2	Respect among student and staff	-0.258**	1.000			
3	Satisfactory pay scales	-0.324**	-0.215**	1.000		
4	Satisfactory promotion avenues	-0.251**	-0.161*	0.056	1.000	
5	Chance to serve different people	-0.036	-0.119	-0.361**	-0.142**	1.000

Notes: (i) * indicates the co-relation Coefficient is significant at 0.05 level of significance; and

(ii) ** indicates the coefficient is significant at 0.01 level of significance.

Author's Calculations

The fifth variable i.e. chance to serve different people is also negatively affected by other four variables and the affect is statistically significant.

(ii) Inter-correlation among the behavioural components of the supervisor to provide job-satisfaction

Table-7 explains the inter-correlation among the

behavioural components of the supervisor to provide job satisfaction. The first variable i.e. the credit by the supervisor for work done is positively and significantly related with the remaining variables except two, i.e., gives the orders which are difficult to carry, the variable credit for work done is positively related but the relationship is statistically insignificant. Similarly, credit for work done given by the supervisor is negatively related with the variable if the supervisor likes or dislikes the flattery. This coefficient is significant at 0.05 level of significance but insignificant at 0.01 percent level of significance.

The second variable of behavioural components of supervisor, i.e., encouragement in depression by the supervisor is also positively correlated with the most of the variables. Here also the same trend as like the first variable is followed.

The third variable, i.e., listening to the difficulties of employee is also positively affected by the other variables. The trend is same as like the first variable but in this case the correlation coefficient with the last variable. i.e., whether the supervisor likes or dislikes the flattery, is negative but insignificant at both five percent and one percent level of significance.

It has been noticed from the Table 7 that first eleven variables are positively related with each other. Including the aforementioned three variables, other eight are: Invites welfare suggestions by the supervisor given by you; respects your skill, ability and efficiency; informs about the library's policies; proper and timely support; welcomes your new ideas; believes employee's welfare as its own welfare; gives order which are difficult to carry and; considering subordinates laborious. All the variables except variable ten (i.e. gives orders which are difficult to follow) and variable eleven (i.e.

Table 7 : Correlation Matrix of 12 × 12 showing inter-correlation among the behavioural components of the supervisor

S. No.	*Variable*	*1*	*2*	*3*	*4*	*5*	*6*	*7*	*8*	*9*	*10*	*11*	*12*
1	Credit for work done	1.000											
2	Encouragement in depression	0.560^{**}	1.000										
3	Listening of difficulties	0.382^{**}	0.606^{**}	1.000									
4	Invites welfare suggestions given by you	0.565^{**}	0.503^{**}	0.450^{**}	1.000								
5	Respects your skill, ability & efficiency	0.670^{**}	0.446^{**}	0.412^{**}	0.677^{**}	1.000							
6	Keeps informed you about library's policies	0.483^{**}	0.477^{**}	0.367^{**}	0.602^{**}	0.610^{**}	1.000						
7	Gives Proper and timely support	0.580^{**}	0.382^{**}	0.350^{**}	0.617^{**}	0.664^{**}	0.533^{**}	1.000					
8	Welcome your new ideas for library improvement	0.516^{**}	0.477^{**}	0.400^{**}	0.664^{**}	0.584^{**}	0.656^{**}	0.650^{**}	1.000				
9	Believes employee's welfare as own welfare	0.460^{**}	0.371^{**}	0.367^{**}	0.540^{**}	0.518^{**}	0.501^{**}	0.620^{**}	0.505^{**}	1.000			

S. No.	Variable	1	2	3	4	5	6	7	8	9	10	11	12
10	Gives orders which are difficult to carry on by you	0.071	0.081	0.098	0.285**	0.169**	0.206**	0.118	0.126	0.245**	1.000		
11	Consider his subordinates laborious	0.307**	0.291**	0.233**	0.401**	0.328**	0.335*	0.319**	0.438**	0.453**	0.431**	1.000	
12	Likes/dislikes flattery by the subordinates	-0.149*	-0.245**	- 0.035	-0.053	-0.108	-0.083	-0.044	0.049	-0.010	0.234**	0.238**	1.000

Table 8 : Inter-correlation Matrix of order showing inter-correlation among the motivation factors for increasing efficiency of work

S. No.	Variable	1	2	3	4	5	6	7	8	9	10	11	12
1	Monetary gains	1.000											
2	Job security	0.507**	1.000										
3	Internal Promotion	0.409**	0.423**	1.000									
4	Good physical requirements	0.358**	0.333**	0.592**	1.000								
5	Working hours	0.343**	0.342**	0.407**	0.401**	1.000							
6	Cordial relation with supervisor	0.460**	0.585**	0.506**	0.462**	0.469**	1.000						
7	Recognition for good work done	0.318**	0.491**	0.459**	0.381**	0.394**	0.645**	1.000					
8	Self esteem	0.476**	0.515**	0.439**	0.473**	0.404**	0.651**	0.566**	1.000				
9	Freedom to ideas to give ideas and action	0.430**	0.402**	0.326**	0.399**	0.429**	0.468**	0.425**	0.557**	1.000			
10	Congenial atmosphere for work	0.430	0.450	0.434	0.423**	0.476**	0.702**	0.629	0.642	0.554**	1.000		

S. No.	Variable	1	2	3	4	5	6	7	8	9	10	11	12
11	Chances for professional development	0.402**	0.437**	0.462**	0.434**	0.425**	0.497**	0.441**	0.520**	0.615**	0.569**	1.000	
12.	Residence near the office	0.256**	0.139**	0.360**	0.295**	0.364**	0.290**	0.197**	0.321**	0.371**	0.411**	0.370**	1.000

Notes: '*' signifies correlation is significant at five percent level of significance.

'**' signifies correlation is significant at ten percent level of significance.

considering the subordinate laborious) are negatively related with 12th variable (likes on dislikes flattery by the subordinates). The aforementioned variables are positively related with the 12th variable as stated earlier.

Hence, it is clear form the empirical examination of Table- 8 that job security and atmosphere for work are positively and significantly related with the perks and other monetary and non-monetary gains.

(iii) Inter-Correlation among the motivator factors for increasing efficiency of Work

In Table- 8, we have the different variables reflecting the benefits from work. These gains are bifurcated among monetary gains and non-monetary gains. Monetary gains are those which can be measured with the measuring rod of money and those which cannot be measured with the measuring rod of money are non-monetary one. The variables (Gains) can be specified as: Monetary gains; Job security; Internal promotion; Cordial relations with supervisor; Recognition for good work done; Self esteem; Freedom of ideas and actions; Congenial atmosphere for work; Chances for professional development; and Residence near the office.

It is evident from the Table-8 that all the variables are statistically significantly correlated with each other at 99 percent level of confidence which means the all types of gains affect positively to other gains. One important trend has been noticed that the job security is positively and significantly related with other motivators, e.g. it is positively related with monetary gains, internal promotion, good physical requirements, working hours, and so on with all other variables. It means as monetary and non-monetary benefits rises, the job satisfaction also rises.

Further an important conclusion can be derived using the variable congenial atmosphere for work (10th variable). The conclusion is that as the monetary and non monetary gains arises, the atmosphere for the work becomes more conducive that results in motivation for employees to improve their productivity at their working hours. The conclusion is that as the monetary and non-monetary gains rise the atmosphere for the work becomes more conducive and motivate the worker to improve her productivity and efficiency during the working hours.

(iv) Inter-correlation among the recruitment and promotion policy variates

Table- 9 contains the correlation coefficient for the recruitment and promotion policy variates. Here we have an important variable of satisfaction from the recruitment policy which is positively related with the other three included variables, i.e.; does the library provide good chances for promotion; partiality in promotion and; justice and honesty in promotion.

The major conclusions drawn from Table- 9 are that the satisfaction from recruitment policy (variable) is positively affected by other three variables, but good prospects for promotion and justice and honesty in promotion are related positively and significantly with aforementioned variables but partiality in promotion and satisfaction from recruitment policy are insignificantly correlated with each other. It means the partiality in promotion does not affect significantly the satisfaction form recruitment policy.

Further analysis of Table-9 reveals that the good prospect for promotion is positively and significantly related with other three variables. Consequently, with the satisfactory recruitment policy, partiality in promotion and honesty in promotion, the prospects for promotion riseses. Overall, we can say that more transparency recruitment policy increases the satisfaction.

Table 9 : Correlation Matrix of showing inter-correlation among recruitment and promotion policy variates

Sr. No.	*Variables*	*1*	*2*	*3*	*4*
1	Satisfaction from recruitment policy	1.000			
2	Good prospects for promotion	0.618**	1.000		
3	Partiality inpromotion	0.110	0.214**	1.000	
4	Justice and honesty in giving promotion	0.422**	0.476**	0.170*	1.000

Notes: (i)* indicates that coefficient is significant at 0.01 level (two tailed); and (ii) ** indicates that coefficient is significant at 0.05 level (two tailed).

Author's Calculations

Similarly, justice and honesty in promotion are also positively related with other factors. It means the better recruitment policy will enhance the justice and honesty in the promotion.

The third variable partiality in promotion is significantly and positively related with the good prospects for promotion but it doesn't affect significantly satisfaction from recruitment policy. The correlation among the partiality in promotion and justice and honesty in promotion is very small i.e. 0.170 which is insignificant at one percent level of significance but significant at five per cent level of significance.

(v) Inter-correlation among the job and family relationship variates:-

In Table-10, we have different variables relating with the family life of the employees. The inter-correlation among these variates is examined. The analysis reveals that there exists positive correlation with passing time pleasantly at home and suitability of rules for a married lady; participation of family in household responsibilities; and encouragement by family to study further. The variables of disturbance due to family problems, family's doings against wishes are negatively correlated with the passing time pleasantly at home.

Table 10 : Inter-correlation coefficient of the job and family relationship variates

Sr. No.	Variables	1	2	3	4	5	6
1	Passing time pleasantly at home	1.000					
2	Family's doings against your wishes	-0.446**	1.000				
3	Suitability of official rules for married lady	0.267*	-0.314	1.000			
4	Disturbance due to family problems	-0.326**	0.305**	-0.194**	1.000		
5	Family's participation in household responsibilities	0.264**	-0.183**	0.108	-0.217**	1.000	
6	Encouragement by family to study further	0.373**	-0.313**	0.127	-0.197**	0.333**	1.000

Notes: (*i*)* indicates that coefficient is significant at 0.01 level (two tailed); and (*ii*) ** indicates that coefficient is significant at 0.05 level (two tailed).

Author's Calculations

Further, family's doings against wishes are positively correlated with disturbance due to family's problems. All other four variates affect negatively the aforementioned variable.

The suitability of the rules for a married lady is negatively associated with disturbances due to family problems and family's doings against wishes. Except these two, all other three variables are positively and significantly associated with the aforementioned variable.

The fifth variable, i.e., family's participation in household responsibilities is negatively associated with the variables of family's doings against the wishes and disturbance due to family problems respectively.

The major conclusion drawn by the analysis of Table-10 is that the family's participation and encouragement is more important to provide conducive environment in the job work. If the family life of the women librarian's is good then she would be satisfied by the job but without the family's encouragement a women employee can not provide healthy environment to the job work, rather it will reduce her efficiency and productivity on the job.

(vi) Inter-correlation among the personal and social factors

The different personal and social factors affecting the job satisfaction have been defined in Table-11. The inter-correlation among these variables have been examined.

The first variable in Table-11 is social and economic independence due to the job. The variable is positively and significantly related with the second variable i.e. empowerment and independence to deal with every kind of social traditions, and third variable i.e. authority to say in decision making at home due to the job. Except these two, the variable one is positively related with eighth variable i.e. help of neighbours at the time of trouble. All other variables are negatively related with first variable.

The same trend has been noticed in case of second variable of empowerment and independence to deal with every kind of social traditions.

The third variable is positively associated with first two variables and last two, i.e., 7th and 8th variable. The negative association of 3rd variable with 4th, 5th and 6th has been noticed. It means the social customs, heartedness at home and caste discrimination etc. negatively affect the women librarians to have a say in decision making at home due to job.

The fourth variable feel hurt even by small incidents on the job is negatively associated with first, second, third and eighth variabl,e but positively associated with all other variables. It means being hurt at home or unssatisfactory family life, the social and economic independence gets reduced.

The 5th variable in Table-11 also follows the same trend as mentioned in earlier paragraph.

The sixth variable is problems due to caste discrimination. This variable also follows the same trend and is negatively associated with first, second, third and eighth variable but positively and significantly associated with other three variables.

The seventh factor i.e. health affect on the progress doesn't have a significant impact or association with other personal and social factors, except the factor 4th i.e. feel hurt even by small incidents at home as well as at job and 8th factor i.e. help of neighbours at the time of trouble.

The major conclusions derived from Table-11 are that the customs, traditions, caste discriminations

Table 11 : Correlation coefficient matrix of order consisting inter-correlation among the personal and social factors affecting job satisfaction

S. No.	Variables	1	2	3	4	5	6	7	8
1	Social and economic welfare due to job	1.000							
2	Empowerment and independence to deal with every kind of social traditions	0.639**	1.000						
3	Authority to say in decision making at home due to job	0.597**	0.557**	1.000					
4	Feel hurted even by small incidents on the job	-0.194**	-0.267**	-0.230**	1.000				
5	Believing most of the social customs are troublesome	-0.152**	-0.159**	-0.130	0.159**	1.000			
6	Problems due to caste discrimination	-0.213**	-0.257**	-0.244**	0.043	0.112	1.000		
7	Health affect on progress	-0.319	-0.087	0.002*	0.199**	0.091	0.142	1.000	

S. No.	Variables	1	2	3	4	5	6	7	8
8	Help of neighbours at the time of trouble	0.203**	0.173*	0.187*	-0.161*	-0.180*	-0.212**	-0.214**	

Notes: '*' indicates coefficient is significant at 5 percent level of significance.

'**' indicates coefficient is significant at 1 percent level significance.

Author's Calculations

etc. social bounds negatively affect the independence of women employees which further hamper the job environment, and satisfaction from the job is low. But if they face encouragement, friendly and conducive family life which is full from satisfaction, always affect positively the job environment. If the job environment is proper it will always provide the satisfaction to the workers.

SECTION-II : FACTORS RESPONSIBLE FOR DISSATISFACTION FROM JOB: A CORRELATION AND STEPWISE REGRESSION BASED ANALYSIS

In this section, we consider the different factors responsible for dissatisfaction from job. These factors are: lack of incentives and recognition for doing good job, staff strength, lack of overall coordination among staff members in the functioning of the library, partial treatment and negligence from authority, lack of in-service training for professional advancement and lack of time for taking higher responsibilities. The inter-corelation and stepwise regression analysis for the factors mentioned in below Table -12 explain the correlational analysis of the mentioning factors affecting the dissatisfaction from the job.

The first factor lack of the incentives and recognition for doing the job is positively related with all other variables responsible for the job satisfaction.

A similar trend has been noticed in case of all other variables included in Table-12. All variables are significantly and positively associated with the other remaining variables.

Thus, it is clear by analyzing Table-12 that if the one factor responsible for dissatisfaction will be effective then it will enhance the effect of other factors too, and the job dissatisfaction will increase among the women

Table 12 : Inter-correlation matrix of order showing the relationship among factors responsible for job dissatisfaction

S. No.	*Variable*	*1*	*2*	*3*	*4*	*5*	*6*	*7*	*8*
1	Lack of incentives and recognition for doing good job	1.000							
2	Staff strength	0.274**	1.000						
3	Lack of overall coordination among staff members	0.165*	0.153*	1.000					
4	Partial treatment and negligence from authority	0.351**	0.283**	0.332**	1.000				
5	Lack of in-service training for professional advancement	0.345**	0.296**	0.266**	0.415**	1.000			
6	Lack of time for taking higher responsibilities	0.282**	0.161**	0.247**	0.415**	0.458**	1.000		
7	Lack of promotion avenues	0.295**	0.186**	0.115	0.331**	0.515**	0.348**	1.000	
8	Service conditions	0.251**	0.273**	0.236**	0.360**	0.188**	0.143*	0.237**	1.000

Notes: '*' refers significance at 5 percent level (two tailed).

'**' refers significance at 1 percent level (two tailed).

Author's calculations

library workers.

An important conclusion drawn by the analysis is that if we have to provide satisfaction to the women library professionals workers then we will have to control the aforementioned factors which are responsible for the dissatisfaction from job.

In further analysis of factors responsible for dissatisfaction from the job among women library professionals, the stepwise regression tool has been applied. In the first step we have lack of promotion avenues as dependent variable and in second step we have service conditions as dependent variable. The variables from serial number 1 to 6 in Table-12 are used as independent variables.

In following regression let us consider the effect of first six variables on lack of promotion activities avenues.

$X_{1i} = 0.454 + 0.094\ X_{2i} + 0.002\ X_{3i} - 0.066\ X_{4i} + 0.96\ X_{5i} + 0.401\ X_{6i} + 0.098\ X_{7i} + U_i$ ...(I)

(3.455) (1.478) (0.031) (-1.107) (1.460) (5.537) (1.529)

In above regression

X_1 = Lack of promotion avenues

X_2 = Lack of incentives and recognition for doing job

X_3 = Staff Strength

X_4 = Lack of overall coordination among staff members in functioning of library

X_5 = Partial treatment and negligence from authority

X_6 = Lack of in-service training for professionalism

X_7 = Lack of time for taking higher responsibilities

U_i = Weight lifting, strain on eyes etc.

It is evident from above equation that lack of

incentives and recognition for doing job (X_2) positively affect the lack of promotion avenues i.e., less incentive will lead to less promotion avenues. The variable staff strength (X_3) also positively affects lack of promotion avenues but the coefficient is insignificant and statistically does not differ significantly from zero.

Lack of overall coordination among staff negatively affects the promotion avenues. The values in brackets are t-values obtained by applying t-statistics. As the sample size is large i.e. n=200, therefore we compare these values with the tabulated value of z at 5% level of significance, i.e., with 1.96. The t value of aforementioned coefficient is 1.07 which is les than 1.96 hence this coefficient is also insignificant.

The variable which is significantly affecting the promotion avenues is lack of in-service training for professionalism. It affects positively lack of promotion avenues. The t value of this coefficient is 5.537 which is very high value as compared to 1.96. The analysis of variance table provides the value of f-statistics equal to 3.971 which confirms the hypothesis that at least one variable included in regression is significant, i.e., statistically differ from zero and the variable is lack of in-service training activities for professionalism. Using R^2, i.e., coefficient of multiple determinants which is equal to 0.281 we can say that due to the independent variables included in regression 28.1 percent variation in the dependent variable is explained and rest 72 percent variation is by chance.

Now, considering the eighth variable service condition as dependent variable which depends upon the same explanatory variables included in the model one, we get the following estimated model:

$$X_{1i} = 0.657 + 0.119\, X_{2i} + 0.162\, X_{3i} + 0.124\, X_{4i} +$$

$0.258\ X_{5i} - 0.020\ X_{6i} - 0.045\ X_{7i} + U_i$ ...(II)
(4.197) (1.578) (2.307) (1.755) (3.298) (-0.235) (-0.589)

Equation (II), explains the positive relationship between lack of service incentives (X_2) and poor service condition, but the coefficient or the effect is insignificant at 5 percent level of significance. The rising staff strength also affects directly the poor service conditions which signify the problem of overstaffing and diminishing return. Lack of overall coordination among the staff member is also positively affecting poor service conditions. All these variables are affecting insignificantly the service conditions.

The partial treatment and negligence from the authority (X_5) is positively affecting the service conditions significantly. It means if the authority will indulge is partiality then it will affect the service conditions adversely. The affect of lack of incentives (X_{3i}) is also significant at 5 per cent level. The variables lack of in-service training for professionalism (X_{6i}) and lack of time for taking higher responsibility (X_{7i}) are negatively affecting the poor service conditions but these coefficients are insignificant at 5 per cent as well as one per cent level of significance. The F value is 7.318 which states at least one variable is significant among the independent variables included in model (II). The R^2 , i.e., coefficient of multiple determined is 0.160 which means in the variable poor service conditions 16 per cent variation is due to the independent variables included in the model. Rest of 84 per cent variation is by chance. i.e., due to those variables which are not included in the model.

SECTION-III : APPLICATION OF FACTOR ANALYSIS TO IDENTIFY SIGNIFICANT FACTORS AFFECTING JOB SATISFACTION

As we encountered the large number of variables in our questionnaire which affect the satisfaction or dissatisfaction on job, it is very difficult to interpret all these factors simultaneously.

The factor analysis can be utilized to examine the underlying patterns or relationships for a large number of variables and determine if the information can be condensed or summarized in a smaller set of factors or components. Using the SPSS version 7.5 software the results pertaining to factor analysis have been calculated for the job satisfaction factor (variables).

The Table-13 explains the factors or components extracted which affect significantly all other variables or which are significantly associated with other variables.

The total variables considered under the heading of factors affecting job satisfaction are: work with good and cooperative persons, work independence, number of working hours, salary in relation to the amount of work done, comparative salary of similar skilled workers, fringe benefits, supporting facilities such as typist equipment etc., job security, impartial attitude of the authority and supervisor's attitude. Among these factors included the first three factors are most significant one and it is clear from the cumulative percentage of variation that out of 100 percent variation, 56.580 per cent variation is due to these three factors extracted.

The most significant factors extracted are work with good and cooperative persons, work independence and number of working hours. These extracted factors explain 20.359, 19.384 and 16.837 per cent variations respectively in the total common variation in factor loads.

The first variable work with nice and cooperative persons is highly positively and significantly related or associated with all other variables. It signifies that if the working circle is good and cooperative, it enhances the work independence. Employees become ready to work for late hours if the work partners are cooperative and friendly. The friendly, benefits, supporting facilities, job security etc. It is because of the positive attitude of the worker towards work.

Table 13 : Factors extracted using factor analysis for the variables concerning with job satisfaction

Sr. No.	*Variables*	*Components Extracted* 1	2	3
1	Work with good and cooperative persons	0.555	0.475	-0.238
2	Work independence	0.442	0.601	-0.230
3	Working hours	0.357	0.569	0.375
4	Salary in relation to the amount of work done	0.626	-0.186	-0.354
5	Comparative salary of similar skilled workers	0.649	-0.135	-0.420
6	Fringe benefits	0.711	-0.104	0.057
7	Supporting facilities such as typist, equipments etc.	0.528	-0.053	0.538
8	Job security	0.504	-0.427	-0.228
9	Impartial attitude of the authority	0.598	-0.346	0.417
10	Supervisor's attitude	0.652	-0.0046	0.207
	Percentage of variance	20.359	19.384	16.837
	Cumulative percentage	20.359	39.743	56.580

Author's Calculations

The second variable i.e. work independence is positively associated with first and third variable but negatively associated with remaining variables. The third variable i.e., number of working hours are positively related with fringe benefits, supporting facilities, impartial attitude of the authority and supervisor's attitude. Except these variables, all other variables are negatively associated with the third variable.

In Table-14 the factor analysis have been further applied to find out most significant factors associated with other factors pertaining to the job situation and satisfaction levels.

The observations from Table-14 explains the most significant factors extracted using the principle component analysis. These four factors are cooperation from male supervisor, cooperation from female supervisor, cooperation from male coworkers and cooperation from female coworkers. These variables explain approximately 74 per cent variation in the whole analysis, rest of the variables are insignificant.

It is evident from the analysis that the most significant factors influencing the satisfaction level are the cooperation of male or female supervisor and cooperation from male or female coworkers.

SECTION-IV : ON-THE-JOB AND OFF-THE-JOB FACTORS AFFECTING JOB SATISFACTION

To test the hypothesis whether on-the-job factors and off-the-job factors differ significantly, we apply the Mann-Whitney non-parametric U-test.

The different types of on-the-job factors are given in the Table 4. All these factors affect the job satisfaction via job and management.

Table 14 : Factors extracted for the variables concerning satisfaction level

Sr. No.	Variables	Factors Extracted 1	2	3	4
1	Cooperation from male supervisor	0.743	-0.114	-0.338	0.190
2	Cooperation from female supervisor	0.693	-1.000	-0.266	0.076
3	Cooperation from male coworker	0.741	-0.278	-0.352	0.164
4	Cooperation from female coworker	0.689	-0.347	-0.376	0.141
5	Cooperation from male subordinate	0.689	0.035	-0.171	-0.525
6	Cooperation from female subordinate	0.654	-0.0003	-0.130	-0.538
7	Team spirit in unit	0.692	-0.340	0.435	0.222
8	Team spirit in library system	0.624	-0.330	0.432	0.279
9	Involvement of staff in transfer, promotion of staff	0.607	-0.140	0.444	-0.268
10	Opportunity to contact with people	0.566	0.508	0.026	0.321
11	Freedom to use own judgement	0.659	-0.0025	0.400	-0.190
12	Chance to guide and help people in getting information	0.593	0.712	0.041	0.058
13	Praise form the users for help and guidance	0.511	0.762	0.032	0.089
	Percentage of variation	22.445	18.445	18.470	14.274
	Cumulative percentage	22.45	41.187	59.657	73.931

Author's Calculations

In the Table 5 off-the-job factors have been discussed. These factors affect the job satisfaction via adjustment in life and social relations. These factors affect the job satisfaction because if due to job the respect of the employee at the family and in social circle rises then the satisfaction from job will increase.

All these factors given in Table 4 and Table 5 are enquired from the women library workers in the form of yes or no. The frequencies pertaining to the percentage of answers in yes out of the 200 cross section units has been compared for 'on-the-job factors' and 'off-the-job factors'.

As the t-test does not compare all the characteristics of two samples therefore, the non-parametric Mann-Whitney U-test has been applied. The U-statistics has been converted into the Z-statistics by applying the following formula

$$z = \frac{U - E(U)}{SE(U)}$$

Where, E(U) is the expected value of U,

SE(U) is the standard error of U-statistics.

The calculated value of Z is then compared with the tabulated value of Z at given level of significance. If the calculated value of Z is less than the tabulated value of Z then the null hypothesis of insignificant difference between two samples is accepted. If calculated value of Z is greater than the tabulated value then the null hypothesis is rejected and we can say both samples, i.e., on the job factors and off the job factors differ significantly.

Using the frequencies assigned to on-the-job factors and off-the-job factors given in Table 4 and Table 5 respectively, we have calculated following values:

$U = 131, \quad N_1 = 32, \quad N_2 = 12$

The calculated value of Z is 1.34 and comparing this value of Z with the tabulated value of Z i.e. 1.96 at 95 percent level of confidence. We conclude calculated value of Z = 1.34 is less than the tabulated value $Z_{0.05}$ = 1.96. Therefore, the null hypothesis of insignificant difference between on the job and off the job factors is accepted.

The analysis or application of Mann-Whitney U-test explains that on-the-job and off-the-job factors samples do not differ significantly. In the job satisfaction both factors are equally important and no one can be ignored.

SECTION-V : EFFECT OF DEMOGRAPHIC FACTORS ON JOB SATISFACTION

To test the effect of demographic factors on the job satisfaction we have applied Logistic Model. The Logistic Model has been particularly selected because of the qualitative nature of the dependent variable. The dependent variable considered here is the overall job satisfaction. In our questionnaire, we have enquired about the overall satisfaction level of women library professionals from the job. The dependent variable Y is defined as

$$Y=\begin{cases}1:\text{for satisfied}\\0:\text{unsatisfied}\end{cases}$$

this variable Y has been regressed upon 10 explanatory variables defined as follows

$$Y=f(X_1,X_2,X_3,X_4,X_5,X_6,X_7,X_8,X_9,X_{10}) \qquad \text{... (III)}$$

Where X_1 = Age in years

X_2 = Experience in years

$$X_3=\begin{cases}1:\text{for married}\\0:\text{for otherwise}\end{cases}$$

$$X_4=\begin{cases}1:\text{if husband occupies a government job}\\0:\text{if husband occupies a private job}\end{cases}$$

X_5 = Number of dependents in family

$$X_6 = \begin{cases} 1\text{:for urban residence} \\ 0\text{:for rural residence} \end{cases}$$

$$X_7 = \begin{cases} 1\text{:nuclear family} \\ 0\text{:Joint family} \end{cases}$$

$$X_8 = \begin{cases} 1\text{:professional qualification} \\ 0\text{:otherwise} \end{cases}$$

$$X_9 = \begin{cases} 1\text{: for the person who get promotion after job} \\ 0\text{ : otherwise} \end{cases}$$

$$X_{10} = \begin{cases} 1\text{: for A class employee} \\ 0\text{ : otherwise} \end{cases}$$

The results for 200 cross sectional units i.e. for 200 employees have been calculated by using the SPSS version 7.8. Table- 15 contains the results pertaining to the Logistic Model applied.

Table 15 : Results pertaining to the Logistic Model applied to obtain the effect of demographic factors on job satisfaction (Y_i)

Predictor	*Estimate coefficients*	*Z-values*	*Decision about H_o*
Constant	0.062	0.05	Accepted
X_1	0.026	0.71	Accepted
X_2	(-) 0.008	-0.23	Accepted
X_3	(-) 0.027	-0.05	Accepted
X_4	(-) 0.248	-0.73	Accepted
X_5	(-) 0.047	-0.12	Accepted
X_6	0.575	1.74	Accepted
X_7	(-) 0.1329	-0.39	Accepted

X_8	0.1637	0.41	Accepted
X_9(-) 0.3541	-1.05	Accepted	
X_{10}(-) 0.192	-0.59	Accepted	

Notes: (*i*) The null hypothesis is Under H_0 : Coefficient is insignificant Against H_1 : Coefficient is significant;

(*ii*) The hypothesis is accepted at both 95% and 99% confidence level

Author's calculations

It is evident from the above Model or Table that age affect the job satisfaction positively. It means with the rising age satisfaction from the job also rises.

Similar trend has been noticed in case of the affect of experience on satisfaction with the rising expertise or experience in job, the satisfaction from the job rises and dissatisfaction falls.

The marital status of the women worker is negatively affecting the satisfaction from job. As the coefficient of X_3 is negative, the results reveal that after marriage the women workers become dissatisfied from the job.

The job/occupation of the husbands of the women workers also negatively affects the satisfaction. The workers whose husbands occupy a public sector or government job are not satisfied by their own job. On the other hand the workers whose husbands are private employee or occupy a private job seem to be satisfied by their current job.

Similarly with the rising number of dependence in the family, the job satisfaction falls. As the coefficient of X_5 is (-0.047), the affect of number of dependents is negative on the job satisfaction. The meaning is straight forward. The rising family sizes increase the expenditure of the family and for a fixed income group, with limited income, it becomes difficult to survive and hence dissatisfaction form the job arises. Also the women employees need more time and energy to tackle domestic affairs. Interest or passion for jobs decreases.

The variable whether women belong to urban areas or rural areas also affects the job satisfaction. It has been noticed that the women living in urban areas are more satisfied by their job as compared to those living in rural areas.

Further, due to the negative sign of the coefficient of X_7 variable, it is evident that women living in nuclear families are dissatisfied with their jobs. On the other hand, women living in joint families are satisfied with their work. The main conclusion drawn is that with the rising number of nuclear families, job satisfaction is falling and dissatisfaction is rising.

An important variable affecting job satisfaction is the qualification. The coefficient obtained has a positive sign, which predict that with the rising number of women with professional qualification, job satisfaction is rising and those who are without the professional qualification feel dissatisfied from their job.

The ninth variable (X_9) that explains the affect of promotion on job satisfaction has negative sign. It exhibits that those women who have get the promotions after joining are rather dissatisfied with their jobs as compared to the women who don't get any promotion and with less professional qualification. This funding is contrary to the commonly held view that promotion increase happiness and satisfaction.

The last variable which has been taken in the sample explaining the variation in the dependent variable of job satisfaction (Y) is the class of the employee (X_{10}). For A class women or employees we have assigned the value one (1) and other women employees with lower classes are assigned the value zero. A negative impact of the A-class has been noticed on the job satisfaction. It has been noticed that the women workers who are working in A-class or with higher pay scales or packages are dissatisfied with their jobs compared with the women working is the lower level jobs.

Although these variables are included into the model but they affect the dependent variable (Y) insignificantly. If we see the column Z of values, then we observe that the coefficients of the entire explanatory variable are insignificant, i.e., the coefficients do not differ statistically from zero. All the Z values are compared with the tabulated value of 1.96 and all the calculated values are less than 1.96 which means the null hypothesis of the insignificant coefficient has been accepted.

Applying the analysis of variance (ANOVA) we obtained the value of F which is also insignificant. Hence, these factors don't explain much variation in the dependent variable of job satisfaction.

SECTION-VI : CONCLUSIONS

The major conclusions drawn from this chapter are:

(i) Cooperation of supervisor, coworkers and subordinates enhance the job satisfaction among the women library workers.

(ii) On-the-job and off-the-job factors both affect the job satisfaction of a woman library professional.

(iii) A woman worker feels satisfied with job if she gains family respect and official respect. The financial or monetary factors hardly matter in the job satisfaction.

(iv) The women library professionals who are on higher positions are dissatisfied with their jobs. This dissatisfaction may be due to the systematic problems in the job administration or may be due to the rising utility of money with rising pay level/ scale.

8

Overview and Trends

As sleep is natural to man so is work. It is the most important social activity of human being, perhaps next to sleep. It spans most of the living time of the individual. Probably next to family, work has become the compact core of human activities. Some of the persons even view that the aim of education is to prepare one for work. Work provides dignity, status, challenge and a sense of achievement to many of us.

In the modern era, job satisfaction has become a major and highly complex problem facing every service oriented organization like libraries.

Library has been termed as a trinity of books, users and library staff. As the teacher is the transmitter and disseminator of knowledge, so it is the librarian. So, librarians have directed relatively more their energies to collect library material than to library personnel. At many fronts and forums, they try to draw the attention of authorities, government and society to this factor.

A library is a service oriented institution and library services depend not only on the collection but equally on library staff. The library staff who makes, develops, organizes and services a collection, is of greater significance. And this constituent of the trinity has unfortunately not arrested the attention of library managers to the extent as it should have.

It is the belief of the investigator that the worker's satisfaction is the basic ingredient of effective organizational behaviour. It is determined by the totality of the work. The organizational structure and climate on the one hand and what employees bring with them to an organization on the other. Their expectancy, need system and response dispositions interact with the organizational variables. The resultant outcome is job satisfaction.

Job satisfaction is vital to the library as well as to those associated with or interacting with libraries. It may not be an exaggeration to say that a library would be what its personnel makes of it.

The summary and major findings of the study are as follows:

The analysis of data collected regarding job satisfaction of women library professionals found no significant difference in the degree of satisfaction caused by on-the-job and off-the-job factors. The findings are based on the different dimensions associated to job satisfaction mentioned in chapter 5.

8.1 LIBRARY PROFESSION

Findings based on perceptions of women library professional for library profession have also included in the beginning of the present chapter 8. Personal attributes/characteristics of women librarians for the original motivation towards librarianship have been revealed by the data acquired by them. The questions under the broad spectrum/heading, "Library profession" included the statements what, why and when the females motivated to this profession.

For the question, why did they opted for library profession showed that the highest percentage is scored by those who claim to have opted it by choice because they are positively attracted to it, i.e. 73 percent, the respondents who'2 came towards it due to circumstances is 23 percent and the remaining four percent refused to disclose the reason for this question.

Majority of the respondents decided to join librarianship after the completion of their academic qualification. 33.5 percent thought about it during their study. Remaining 6 percent subjects came towards it when they were engaged in some other private job. It would be worth mentioning that the 6 percent persons may not be satisfied by their jobs in other sectors due to which they need to join the profession of library.

When asked what attracted and motivated those more to join the profession, majority of the respondents i.e., 31 percent said, there was better bjob prospects. Job attraction came second in rank i.e., 27 percent while unfortunately 16.5 percent people came to the profession only for employment, as there was no other job for them. About 9.5 percent people were motivated to the profession due to good salary. Most of the new entrants i.e., 2 percent subjects have no idea about the nature and value of library profession. They are encouraged, motivated and guided by many people in their contacts to join this profession. In the present study, most of the female entrants i.e., 48.6 percent were guided by their parents. Some of them were followed by friends, i.e., 23.5 percent and those who were guided to join this profession i.e. 12 percent. Some about 8.2 percent were motivated by the teachers towards librarianship. It is clear that about 3/4th of the people have joined this profession by choice and majority were guided by their parents as they thought there are better job prospects here.

The question asked was if the librarianship has turned out to be a right selection by you? In other words, has the profession matched your expectations or not? Regarding the rethinking of respondents, 81.6 percent respondents/librarians were happy over the choice of profession. They gave common statement that librarianship is a female profession. This statement is also reflected in the writings of many authors. So, majority of respondents indicated the right selection of this profession. But unfortunately, 18.4 percent thought that they made a mistake in joining this profession. The cause behind such thinking is the lack of promotion, growth opportunities, lack of incentives and perks, etc. No recognition for their hard work is also one of the major cause behind their dissatisfaction.

It means that majority of people are happy and satisfied as only negligible percent age of people i.e., 18.4 showed dissatisfaction for this factor. The analysis of data showed that out of 200 respondents, 27.6 percent thought of joining many other professions before joining librarianship namely banking, teaching, nursing, social welfare, marketing etc. it revealed that they were also interested to enter other professions. It is very interesting to note that 72.4 percent showed their keen interest to join the library profession at the beginning as the first choice but now out of this number, 1/3rd people are dissatisfied due to many reasons.

To the question of changing the profession with same monetary gains, it is obtained that significant majority of respondent i.e., 57.5 percent revealed that they are not willing to change their present profession with the same monetary perks. It is very healthy and quite satisfactory aspect that majority of respondents appear to be settled until they retire. It revealed their satisfaction on the job. On the other hand, those who wanted to change the job as soon as they got another job are 42.5 percent. They stated many reasons for their dissatisfaction as they were not being recognized, not rewarded, not promoted and got no respect from seniors. If we deeply think and analyze, we come to know that specially in university libraries, junior staff is not satisfied and perhaps they feel that due to the shortage of staff, consequently heavy work load, no chances of promotion etc. create dissatisfaction. And in some cases, respondents are not in such position to take (avail) leave at their own determination. For the question would you recommend to others your profession for early employment? It is evident from data that half of the total respondents i.e., 50 percent have no hesitation to recommend their library profession to other as a place of early employment but 50 percent have negative approach to this. The reason they have stated is that their own family members got no permanent job even after getting post-graduation in Library Science and they are wandering here and there to seek an appropriate job with adequate salary. Moreover, jobs are neither lucrative nor attractive otherwise for a long hour. Equally similar is a response regarding the status of library profession in the eyes of others. About 80 percent thought that this profession is respectable and they get due respect while 20 percent do not think so. The reason they stated that librarians are doing mere clerical job of issue and return of books. Their jobs are not skilled or technical. In some institutions, new librarians are asked to do some other jobs in addition to their library hours. It includes teaching, clerical work or some other work for the management especially in college library.

It is very interesting to note that majority of the respondents, i.e., 61.4 percent are very much interested in this profession. They stated that they are fond of books and want to gain more knowledge and have an urge to serve the people. They joined librarianship by choice. But 38.6 percent answered in negative due to many reasons such as stagnation in promotion eve after having good academic record as well as professional record, unsatisfactory working conditions, less salary for the work done and non-cooperation. It revealed that they are totally dissatisfied. They will never adopt this profession in case they get a chance to start their career again.

In the last, the respondents were asked to give ranks for the five statements which indicated their original motivation to stick to this profession i.e., means of livelihood; satisfactory pay scales; better chances for career making; professional charm; lack of other job in employment market etc.

The data presented in bar charts that the foremost factors which motivate to stick to the library profession is means of livelihood and pay scales respectively and the remaining factor as compared to others get least ranks. (See Bar Chart no. 1).

Among the most important conditions of job satisfaction, the factor "respect for status" gets highest rank and communication between the authorities and staff gets lowest rank as compared to others. (See Bar Chart no. 2).

Among the factors responsible for job satisfaction, the factor named nobility of profession gets higher rank as compared to other ranks. Satisfactory promotion avenues get the least rank. (See Bar Chart no. 3).

Promotion is the most important factor for job

satisfaction but data revealed that this factor showed dissatisfaction among women librarians because they are not satisfied and there is stagnation in their promotion. Among the factors related to their promotion, absence of career path planning gets highest priority as compared to other factors. (See Bar Chart no. 4).

In view of the respondents, highest ranking for the status of profession is given by their family members, while the public at large treats the librarian's status with average rank. Academics are divided over the status/respect given to the librarians.

To conclude, we can say that the majority of the women library professionals are satisfied in this profession and are happy to become a librarian. This attitude and satisfaction can lead to some good performance and contribution to the library profession.

8.2 JOB SATISFACTION

Results are based upon the different factors/ variables associated to job satisfaction under the two broad headings on-the-job factors and off-the job factors. On-the-job factors (32) and off-the-job factors (12) were formulated to measure the job satisfaction level of women working in libraries.

8.2.1. On-the-Job Factors

On-the-job factors included variation and nature of job, cooperation, independence, working conditions, salary and perks, and promotion avenues etc.

Majority of the respondents i.e., 49 percent stated that they were able to keep themselves busy in the job all the time because their job is interesting. 34 percent stated their job as simple routine because they acquired no chance to do different works. 11 percent stated their job challenging while 55 percent felt their work bit boring.

It has been observed that 87 percent of the respondents rated job security on number one. It may be noted that under the job security act, even the employees working in affiliated and aided colleges, are covered by the job security act. Judicial courts and labour courts are always particular about the security of workers. So, the management and the employers do not terminate the services of the employees without proper and complete evidence. Hence, this factor did not matter much with the confirmed employees. But it will matter in the days when the people are hired on contract basis.

The second highly valued parameter is cooperation from the supervisor. 80 percent have mentioned that they get cooperation from the supervisor. It is very important for job productivity and satisfaction. I think that rest of the 20 percent who are not having cooperation may due to personal reasons.

Job variation has been ranked at 3rd position with 75 percent. It is very positive approach because workers learnt different jobs and have exposure to different jobs and different skills. It develops confidence and better understanding of the institutional work. It also saves employees from boredom and burnout.

The other factor having the same rank i.e., 3rd is fringe benefits. It is also very important than the regular salary, fringe benefits should be increased to motivate and satisfy the employees.

The other factors to which the respondents have values are supervisor's attitude 73.1 percent, supporting facilities 70.6 percent, salary 69 percent, in service training for professional development 70.4

percent and the security of female staff 68.8 percent etc. The factors which have got middle ranks are independence 66.3 percent impartiality 60 percent, working conditions 55 percent, work load 44 percent. Psychology and sensitivity which includes hurt with small incidents on job i.e. 44.8 percent, work with unpleasant people, tiredness i.e. 31 percent and anxiety 32 percent etc.

The factors which are least preferred are incentives and recognition 30 percent, lack of promotion avenues 44 percent, justice in giving promotions 30 percent, and individual identity 25 percent and lack of professional development i.e., 70.4 percent. These are the most important factors which create job satisfaction but it is very distressing that women workers showed their dissatisfaction with these factors.

Junior staff feels that there are few avenues for theirb continuing education. Authorities do not pay or encourage them to keep and motivate for further training or continue their professional development. More than 60 percent feel that there are no good chances for their promotion, despite the fact they are sufficiently qualified.

Women professionals suffer in promotions because of their relative lack of mobility. Having worked as a junior staff member, it was inner feeling of investigator to meet junior staff in the libraries. While meeting the junior staff for this study and also talking to them at different forums, the investigator gathered the impression that many of the junior staff complained and quoted instances where less qualified persons with less experienced were holding better positions in university libraries due to personal pulls and bias of authorities. This is a great handicap in promotion and status in this profession.

This inequity experienced by the junior staff affected their overall attitudes and job satisfaction.

The following comments by some junior respondents speak adequately of their frustrations:

"It would have been better if I had stayed in the teaching instead of coming to this low profession. Now I would have been principal of the school".

Some of the juniors were reported to be working on the same past for more than 15 year. After working between 16-22 years in this profession, they are still library assistants, library restorers etc. No promotion, and even no future chances were lamented by the junior respondents.

The younger generation, who were well qualified and entered the profession recently, with probably high expectations had to face tough competition in view of the employment conditions in the libraries.

The juniors perhaps felt as one of them has put it that professionally qualified and experienced staff at the lower level should be well looked after, they are large in number. They should be given chances to attend seminars, and other professional activities for their advancement.

Thus, the juniors were probably in more unfavourable situations which were responsible for their job dissatisfaction.

8.2.2. Off-the-job Factors

Off-the-job factors are concerned with personal and family life. The analysis or application of Mann-Whitney non parametric U-test explains that on-the-job and off-the-job factors associate to concerned samples do not differ significantly. For job satisfaction both factors are equally important and no one can be ignored.

Results have also been presented regarding off-the-job factors. So far as off-the-job factors are concerned, highly ranked factor i.e., 91.2 percent is pleasantly passing time at home. Congenial atmosphere at home creates full satisfaction at job. Then the other equally ranked factors are improvement in qualification is 86.5 percent and the economic independence due to job is 85.6 percent. It is fact that economic independence leads the power for decision making at home. Women librarians with decision making power make up to 83 percent. And the next factors that showed satisfaction is neighborhood i.e., 78.9 percent.

The factors which showed dissatisfaction are caste discrimination in the society and worry about family health and their own health also.

The highly dissatisfied factor ranked 85.3 percent i.e., non cooperation from family members. It is very negative finding which affects seriously on the job productivity and satisfaction of women workers because they could not give fruitful results to the institution without the cooperation of family and colleagues on the job.

To know whether on-the-job factors and off-the-job factors associated to women library professionals working in universities and colleges differ significantly or not, we have applied F-test. Generating Frequency tables for on-the-job factors and off-the-job factors, we calculated variability (variance) of the factors answered by the university and college staff.

8.2.3. Comparative Analysis

Comparative analysis between the women

librarians working in universities and colleges has also been presented. The results of F-test for on-the-job factors provides that F=2.546 for V_1=31 and V_2=11 degrees of freedom. The null hypothesis of insignificant differences between university and college staff is not rejected. Same findings are supported by the off-the-job factors in which the calculated value of F is 1.384. In the lieu of above results, therefore, we concluded that there is no need of separate study to compare job satisfaction and analyze job satisfaction of university and college staff working in libraries separately with the on-the-job factors and off-the-job factors which are the most determinants of job satisfaction.

8.2.4. Co-relational Analysis

Co-relational analysis had also been made on the basis of acquired data. The major conclusions drawn are: a) Cooperation of supervisor, coworkers and subordinates enhances the job satisfaction among the women workers working in the libraries; b) on-the-job and off-the-job factors both affect the job satisfaction for a woman worker; c) a woman worker feels satisfied with job if she gains family respect and official respect. The financial or monetary factors hardly matter in the job satisfaction. If the employee gains promotions etc. or any sort of appreciation for her work, it enhances the official respect via improving the status of the work. The appreciation, therefore, provides more job satisfaction. The factors responsible for stagnation in promotion has been examined and absence of career path planning has been identified as foremost factor; and d) the workers who are on higher positions are dissatisfied with their jobs. This dissatisfaction may be due to the systematic problems in the job and library administration or may be due to the rising utility of money with rising pay level. Shortage of staff and extra work load for the women workers working at higher positions may be the cause of their dissatisfaction. It is, therefore, recommended, that the vacant posts should be filled by the university and college administrators. If the recruitment is not economically feasible, then the students working under the scheme of "Earning while Learning" should be absorbed to do the extra work; e) there also exists positive relationship between job satisfaction and age. Several studies show that job satisfaction increases with age. It is apparent as well as that professional experience and its associated remarks increase with rising age and that one has greater financial resources at one's disposal. The higher position leads to the greater career length and greater career length, higher the level of job satisfaction.

8.2.5. Personal Data of the Women Library professionals under study

In our study, majority of women library staff in their mid career between the ages 41-50 years are satisfied with their jobs while youngest i.e., between 21-30 and the oldest i.e., above 51 years are satisfied because it has been seen that after 50 years of age, people start thinking about their retirement and devote much time to the education and career of their children. So, they are less evolved with the professional work.

Overwhelming majority of respondents i.e., 81 percent are married and 19 percent are unmarried. The reason of such difference is that in the recent years, more of young females are entering the library profession and the profession has become female oriented.

It is clear from Table 1 concerned to age that the percentage of respondents in the age group of 21 – 30 years is right age for marriage according to our culture. It may be mentioned here that only a negligible percentage of respondents is divorced or under some other complications or disputes and they placed themselves as unmarried.

Since library profession is a service profession so majority of the married women i.e., 43 percent have husbands with government jobs. They have regular and steady income. It makes them secure and it is a major factor for their job satisfaction.

It is interesting to note that it is a profession of the urbanities. Rural background librarians make only 23 percent. It may also be due to fact that in the rural areas no adequate career guidance is provided nor there are libraries. As per information ascertained even respondents born in rural areas are also settled and working in the libraries of urban areas.

Going with the trend of the urban environment, overwhelming majority i.e., 76.5 percent of the respondents belongs to nuclear families, and rest of the respondents i.e., 23.5 percent have joint families. There is much difference found for family aspect. Women belonging to nuclear families have less burden and family responsibilities.

Nuclear families are small and have fewer children. In our case, 66 percent respondents have three or less than three children. Therefore, they have comparatively more time for their professional work. Rest of the respondents have more than three children plus their other family members. Naturally, their expenditure will be high and they are not fully satisfied.

Women library professionals of rural areas have

to work in some libraries under very trying and complex conditions. The college campus in many cases is miles away from the city. In the absence of provision of accommodation for library staff in the campus, they have to commute daily from far off places by local transport. In some colleges library is kept open for longer hours. And the women working in the libraries cover a long distance to reach home and the office. So due to the residential problem, they are the worst sufferers. Due to this problem they feel very dissatisfied. Authority should compensate them in one way or the other. It should always keep in mind that women professionals should be treated with a humane touch with more sympathy and understanding their problems.

Majority of the respondents i.e., 65 percent are post graduate degree holders while only 4 percent have Ph.D. in social sciences and all respondents are graduates.

In an interdisciplinary subject like library science post graduation degree holders can give better services and have higher level of job satisfaction. Data revealed that young are better qualified than aged as it should be because to cope with the rising and demanding services and with the changing environment of the libraries.

It is very encouraging and healthy hand in our profession that 15 percent women have passed NET and even 8 percent women library professionals have doctorate degrees in library science but very distressing thing counts that they got no promotion, and feel there is no chance for it as stated by them. Authorities should take into consideration this by giving promotion to qualified ones on the base of qualification and experience. On the other hand, time scale promotion should also be provided to less qualified women on the basis of professional experience etc. Naturally this factor creates dissatisfaction among the women respondents concerned to this study.

Communication is important to both for individual performance and individual satisfaction. It affects attitude to work. Some respondents have deplored the state of affairs in this regard and comment: "There is no process of communication among the employees and administration." They are not at all ready to take into confidence their colleagues." "Consultation among the staff, meetings etc. are not at all applicable in the library.

Better opportunities for having their views considered were enjoyed by some of the seniors women staff involved in management and administration it seems. Attitude of junior female staff was less favourable than that of senior female staff. The juniors think quite different from the seniors in this respect.

Improvement in qualification whether (academic or professional) is an index of job satisfaction. Most of the people want to grow and improve after joining the job. This is mostly done by improving and adding to their academic and professional qualification. In a technical profession like librarianship, it happens quite often because library staff sit in the amidst of books and libraries provide encouraging atmosphere for study.

From the data collected that 38 percent are self motivated and they have inner urge for improving their professional as well as their academic qualification.

On the other hand, majority i.e. 49.5 percent of respondents had improved their qualification due to some administrative conditions put upon them such as for their promotion and annual increments or some other additional responsibilities.

12.5 percent did not improve their qualification for various reasons such as work load, health and family problems etc. It may also be mentioned that they have no charm to raise the living standard of their family because their dissatisfaction from job severely affects their homely atmosphere.

Data revealed that more females have joined in this profession during the recent years. This is a profession which attracts females in a large number. It can also be verified from the current admission enrollment in library and information science departments in Punjab and Delhi universities.

8.2.6. Professional Development

Some other factors based according to the changing environment which create job satisfactions are highlighted separately in the Table 13 of chapter 7. The factors related to the professional development of women librarians revealed their perceptions of the various factors associated to their job satisfaction and scope of further advancement in library profession.

Ever since, machines began to supplant human skills, people have failed to desire adequate pleasure from their work and have been deprived of their work and their sense of pride in the job they do. Employees have therefore been steadily alienated from their jobs and consequently feel unfulfilled.

Use of computers in libraries is very vital but the old women have difficulty in working on computers. An employee who cannot works with computers cannot be considered fit for a modern library. But the present study found that almost 55 percent women librarians have training in computers. It is not a good indicator of job satisfaction who do not know computers. While it is admitted by 64 percent that computers have impact on work and job satisfaction.

The 51 percent respondents without the knowledge/training in computer wanted facilities for in service computer training. It would enable them to enhance their professional competence. So, they should acquire knowledge in computers to work efficiently.

Membership of professional associations is the indicator of zeal for library profession. It is necessary for the librarians to involve in different activities of professional development such as awareness of the latest developments in the profession by reading professional literature, holding of membership in different professional organizations, participating in conferences, seminars, workshops, refresher courses and contributing to professional knowledge in the form of books and articles in order to become successful practitioner and thereby raising the status of library profession.

The extent of involvement of library staff in the above said activities for professional development revealed their professional zeal and interest for the profession.

But it has been found that the membership of women librarians in the professional associations is very small i.e., only 26.5 percent only. Majority of the respondents were not holding membership of an association.

Only 36 percent respondents attend seminar, conference, workshops etc. and avail financial assistance and duty leave. 28 percent have articles in publications (published work).

The respondents deprived of these activities

showed grievances/grudge against the authority. They are not being permitted to attend professional activities. Only seniors get this chance. Most junior staff showed dissatisfaction. Naturally there was a feeling of discrimination. It is very essential for the authorities to take into consideration all these factors to keep the women staff up to date with their professional advancement by providing equal opportunities to library staff.

These finding indicate that the individuals perceive different degrees of job satisfaction with respect to the same job characteristics, depending upon their expectations and values determined by their experience and adaptability to their conditions in work-life. The different studies covered in literature review pointed out that any job factor could cause satisfaction, dissatisfaction, or indifference depending upon many situational, contingent, and moderator variables, and job satisfaction was not an absolute process but relative to the alternative available to an individual.

There is no panacea, no magic wand which will transform alienated individuals into happy, contented, hard working, high-quality and high quantity producers, and it is true of job satisfaction as of any other sphere of life that one man's meat is another man's poison. Nevertheless, in the wake of findings of this study, it is recommended that managerial attitudes, approaches and policies be directed towards organizing and motivating the efforts of individuals by creating the appropriate type of work climate that will enable them to achieve their personal/desired goals and have a sense of satisfaction their work. The supervisory climate of the job environment should also be healthy which is conducive to the exercise of the individual's initiative and professional judgment and the librarian's experience of mastery a job.

References

1. Abifarin, F.P. (1992). Personnel attributes and job satisfaction in Nigerian University Libraries. *African Journal of Academic Librarianship, 10*, 19-25.
2. Aggarwal, C.M. (2005). *Pratibimb: Images of Indian womenhood. Vol.1*. Delhi: Indian Publishers and Distributors.
3. Aina J.O. (2004). Leadership skills of women librarians in West Africa. *International Library Movement, 25*, 65-70.
4. Alao, I. A. (1992). The status of job satisfaction among library assistants in four Nigerian academic institutions. *African Journal of Academic Librarianship, 10*, 3-11.
5. Ang, J. and Koh, S. (1997). Exploring the relationships between users information satisfaction and job satisfaction. *International Journal of Information Management, 17*, 169-77.
6. Awasthi, N. (2002). Stress and burnout among library professionals in the universities and colleges of Punjab, Haryana and Chandigarh. *Library Hearld, 40*, 75-86.
7. Banks, J. (1991). Motivation and effective management of library assistants in academic

libraries. *Journal of Library Administration, 14*, 133-154.

8. Barkar, R.M. (1995). The interaction between end user computing levels and job motivation and job satisfaction: An exploratory study. *Journal of End User Computing, 7*, 12-19.
9. Barlett, C. (2000). Supervisory Communication and subordinate job satisfaction: The relationship between supervisor's staff disclosure, offers of help, offers of cooperation, frequency of contact, trust and subordinate's job satisfaction. *Public Library Quarterly, 18*, 9-30.
10. Beach, D.S. (1965). *Personnel: The management of people at work.* London: Collier Macmillan.
11. Beena, C. and Poduval, P.R. (1988). Relationship of intrinsic and extrinsic motivational factors with job satisfaction of library professionals and R&D professionals. *Kelpro Bulletin, 2*, 56-58.
12. Best, J.W.and Kahn J.V. (1986). *Research in education.* New Delhi: Prentice Hall.
13. Bogdan, R. and Taylor S.J. (1975). *Introduction to qualitative research methods: A phenomenological approach to the social science.* New York: John Wiley.
14. Bullock, R.P. (1952). *Social factors related to job satisfaction.* Columbus: Bureau of Business Research, Ohio State University.
15. Bundy, A. (1988). Job satisfaction of subject librarians in British and Australian polytechnics. *Australian College Libraries, 6*, 24-28.
16. Burgess, C.F. (1982). Job satisfaction of librarians and cataloguers of librarians and cataloguers. *Australian Academic and Research Libraries, 13*, 73-81.

17. Burgess, R.G. (1985). *Issues in educational research: Qualitative methods.* London: The Fahner Press.
18. Bushan Lal (1984). *Factors related to employee performance: A study of library organizations.* Ph.D. Thesis. III, Delhi.
19. Carr Saunders, A.M. and Wilson, P.A. (1937). World population. In Anil Saxena (2006), *Encyclopedia of social welfare* (p.137): New Delhi: SBS publishers and Distributors Pvt. Ltd.
20. Chand, M.P. (2003). Changing status of women and libraries in India. *Herald of Library Science, 42*, 208.
21. Chopra, K. (1984). Job satisfaction among the librarians of Lucknow city. *Herald of Library Science, 23*, 156-161.
22. Chrisman, L.G. (1975). *An analysis of the cataloguer's role within the academic library organization.* Dissertation. Indian University, Graduate Library School.
23. Chwe, S.S. (1976). *A comparative study of librarian's job satisfaction and reference librarians.* Unpublished Dissertation. University of Pittsburg.
24. Clow, D. (1986). French library and information careers. *Journal of Librarianship, 18*, 113-132.
25. D'Elia, G.P. (1979). Determinants of job satisfaction among beginning libraries. *Library Quarterly, 49*, 283-302.
26. Dabas, K.C. (2001). *Application of total quality management to the university libraries in Punjab, Haryana and Chandigarh.* Ph.D. Dissertation, Guru Nanak Dev University.
27. Das Gupta, K. (1998). Women as managers of

libraries: A development process in India. *IFLA Journal, 24*, 245-249.

28. Dawis, R.V. (1974). Describing organisations as reinforcer systems: A new use for job satisfaction and employee attitude surveys. *Journal of Vocational Behaviour, 4*, 32-78.
29. Demers, D.P. (1994). Effect of organizational size on job satisfaction of top editors at U.S. dailies. *Journalism Quarterly, 71*, 914-925.
30. Devi, L.U. (1982). *Status and employment of women in India*. Delhi: B.R. publishing corporation.
31. Doyle, R.G. (1994). Job satisfaction levels of U.S. and International College and University media specialists. *College and University Media Review, 1*, 89-96.
32. Edem, U.S. and Lawal, O.O. (1999). Job satisfaction and publication output of librarians in Nigerian Universities. *Library Management, 20*, 39-46.
33. Estabrook, L. and Bird, C. (1990). Job satisfaction: Does automation make a difference? *Journal of Library Administration, 13*, 175-194.
34. Fisher, D. (1996). Techno stress and the librarian: A critical discussion . *Education Libraries Journal, 39*, 9 -14.
35. Ganguli, H.C. (1971). Industrial Psychology research in India, 1920-1969. *Indian Journal of Industrial Relations, 6*, 223-276.
36. Garg, B.S. (1986). *Personality and job satisfaction of librarians of universities of Delhi and Rajasthan: A multivariate analysis*. Ph.D. Dissertation. University of Rajasthan.

37. Garg, B.S. (1999). Determinants of job satisfaction of librarians: A multivariate analysis. *Journal of Library and Information Science, 24*, 108-123.

38. Garrison, D. (1979). *Apostles of culture: The public librarian and American society*, 1876-1920, New York: The Free Press.

39. Geeson, R. and Goulding, A. (1999). Split personalities: The job satisfaction of learning centre support staff at a multi-site university. *New Review of Academic Librarianship, 5*, 7-22.

40. Ghosh, B.N. (1982). *Scientific method and social research.* New Delhi: Sterling.

41. Gibran, K. (1966). *The prophet.* London: William Heineman.

42. Good, C.V. and Scates, D.E. (1954). *Methods of research.* New York: Appleton Century Craft, Inc.

43. Goode, W.J. and Hatt, P.K. (1952). *Methods in social research.* New York: McGraw-Hill.

44. Goulding, A. (1995). I want to work with books and people: The job satisfaction of public library support staff. *Public Library Journal, 10*, 71-74.

45. Greene, W.H. (2003). *Econometric analysis* (5th ed.). Delhi: Pearson Education.

46. Gundel, R. (1989). The advancement of women in libraries : A subject for women's career. *Buch and Biblioteck, 41*, 445-447.

47. Gupta, A. (2006). *Scholastic achievement in relation to popularity of adolescent students.* M.Ed. Thesis: Guru Nanak Dev University.

48. Gupta, K. (1983). *A study of frustration among working women in relation to their needs, levels of aspiration and some background variables.* M.Ed. Thesis: Kanpur University.

49. Hall, S. (1999). Job satisfaction and absentecism. British Library. *Research and Innovation Report, 166*, 258-261.

50. Halloran, J.K. (1978). *Applied human relations: An organizational approach.* New Delhi: Prentice Hall.

51. Haridasan, S. and Sultan, T. (2002). Occupational stress and burn out among the library staff of Gorakpur University. A study. *Journal of Library and Inforamtion Science, 27*, 41-51.

52. Hariharan, S.V. and Ganeshan, S. (2003). *Participative management and organizational effectiveness.* Delhi: B.R. Publishing Corporation.

53. Harris, R.M. and Tague, J.M. (1989). Reaching the top in Canadian Librarianship: A bibliographical study of sex difference in career development. *Library Quarterly, 59*, 116-130.

54. Heim, K.M. (1987). Men at work their way up: Reasons for status difference between men and women librarians. *Buch and Bibliothek, 39*, 41-45.

55. Hoppock, R. (1935). *Job satisfaction*, New York: Harper and Row.

56. Horenstein, B. (1993). Job satisfaction of academic librarians: An examination of the relationship between satisfaction, faculty status and participation. *College and Research Libraries, 54*, 255-269.

57. Houser, J.D. (1927). *What the employer thinks.* Cambridge Mass. Harvard University Press.

58. Hovekamp, T.M. (1995). Unionization and job satisfaction among professional library employees in academic research institutions. *College and Research Libraries, 56*, 341-350.

59. ILO (1991), *Women at work: Protection of working mothers. An ILO global survey 1964-1984*. Geneva: International labour office.

60. India: Ministry of Education (1974), *Towards equality: A report of the National Committee on the Status of women in India.* New Delhi: Department of Social Welfare.

61. *International Encyclopedia of Social Sciences* (1968). Edited by David L. Sills, Vol. 13,USA: MacMillan.

62. Jain, M.K. (2005). *Research methodology and statistical techniques.* New Delhi: Shree Publishers and Distributors.

63. Jones, O. (1996). Human resources, scientists and internal reputation: The role of climate and job satisfaction. *Human Relations, 49*, 269-294.

64. Jordan, P (1995). *Staff management in library and information work* (3rd ed.). Hamphire: Gover House.

65. Kapoor, A.L. (1982). Motivation among the professional library staff of Delhi University Library System: A case study. *Library Herald, 20*, (2-4):

66. Kapoor, P. (1974). *The Changing status of working women in India.* New Delhi: B.R. Publishing Company.

67. Kaula, P.N. (2004). *Changing dimensions of library and information services in India.* Agra: Y.K. Publishers.

68. Kaur, G. (2005). *Women and the law.* New Delhi: Shree Puiblishers and Distributors.

69. Khandelwal, P. (2003). Job satisfaction. ***In*** M.S. Saiyadain (Ed.), *Organisational behaviour* (pp.). New Delhi: Tata McGraw Hill.

70. Khanna, J.K. (1981). *Personnel management in libraries.* New Delhi : Ess Ess :

71. Koening, M. and Morrison, R. (1996). Faculty status for library professionals: its effect of job turnover and job satisfaction among university research library directors. *College and Research Libraries, 57,* 295-300.

72. Kothari, C.R. (1999). *Research methodology: Method and techniques.* New Delhi: Wiley Eastern.

73. Kumar, K. (1992). Working women and the family. ***In*** Najma Heptulla (Ed.), Reforms for women: Future options (pp.). New Delhi: Oxford.

74. Kumar, PSG (1975). Women and librarianship. *Herald of Library Science, 14,* 221-224.

75. Kumari, Y.K. and Rao, B.S. (2005). *Empowerment of women and rural development.* New Delhi: Serials.

76. Landry, M.B. (2000). Effects of life satisfaction and job satisfaction on reference librarians and their work. *Reference and User Services Quarterly, 40,* 166-177.

77. Lawler, E.E. and Porter, L.W. (1968). What job attitudes tell about motivation. *Harvard Business Review, 46,* 116-124.

78. Leckie, G.J. and Brett, J. (1997). Job satisfaction of Canadian university librarians: A national survey. *College and Research Libraries, 58,* 31-47.

79. Likert, R. (1961). *New pattern of management.* New York: McGraw Hill.

80. Louw, A. (1989). Women in management positions in the library and information services of South Africa. *South African Journal of Library and*

Information Science, 57, 305-309.

81. Lynch, B.P. and Verdin, J.A. (1983). Job satisfaction in libraries: A relationship of the work itself, age, sex occupation group, tenure, supervirary level, career commitment and library department, *Library Quarterly, 53*, 434-447.
82. Lynch, B.P. and Verdin, J.A. (1987). Job satisfaction in libraries: A replication. *Library Quarterly, 57*, 190-202.
83. Marchant, M.P. (1970). *The effects of the decision-making process and related organizational factors in alternative measures of performance in university libraries*. Dissertation. University of Michigan, School of Education.
84. Mathur, K. (2000). *Role of women in management*. Jodhpur: Book Treasure.
85. Mc Doneel, Kata (2009). Surveying the field: the research model of women in librarianship 1882-1898. *Library Quarterly*, 79(3), 279-300.
86. McFarlin, D.B. and Rice, R.W. (1992). The role of facet importance as a moderate in job satisfaction process. *Journal of organizational behaviour, 13*, 41-54.
87. McGregor, D. (1960). *The human side of enterprise*. New York: McGraw Hill.
88. McNally, P.F. (1983). Participation, satisfaction and quality of reference service in Canadian public libraries. *APLA Bulletin, 46*, 65-67.
89. Mehta, R. (2006). *Women executives in the service sector: A study of attitudes, challenges and opportunities*. Unpublished Ph.D. Thesis: Guru Nanak Dev University.
90. Memoria, C.B. and Gankar, S.V. (2003). *Personnel*

Management: Test and Cases (23rd ed.). Mumbai: Himalaya.

91. Ministry of labour, Govt. of India (1988). *Social economic conditions of women workers in industries. A report.* New Delhi.

92. Mirkfakharai, M.H. (1991). Correlates of job satisfaction among academic librarians in the United States. *Journal of Library Administration, 14*, 117-131.

93. Mishra, A.D. (1994). *Problems and prospects of working women in urban India.* Ed. 1. New Delhi: Mittal.

94. Morita, I.T. (1991). Job satisfaction and the changing role of cataloguers. *Journal of Educational Media and Library Science, 28*, 428-432.

95. Morse, N. (1953). *Satisfaction in the white collar job.* Ann Arbour : Institute of Social Research.

96. Morse, N. and Weiss, R. (1981). The functions and meaning of work and the job. *American Sociological Review, 1955* quoted by C.B. Handy. Understanding organizations. Harmondsworth: Midd lesse Penguin.

97. Morse, N.C. and Reimer, R.E. (1956). The experimental change of a major organizational variable. *Journal of Abnormal psychology, 52*, 120-129.

98. Nandy, S.G. (1985). Job satisfaction of the library professionals. *Herald of Library Science, 24*, 296-300.

99. Nandy, S.G. (1988). Job satisfaction of library professionals. *Herald of Library Science, 27*, 210-215.

100. Navalani, K. (1984). *Manpower management in university libraries in India: A survey of job satisfaction*. Ph.D. Dissertation. Dharwad: Karnataka University.

101. Navalani, K. (1990). Job characteristics of library and information work as satisfiers and dissatisfiers: A survey. *Annals of Library Science and Documentation, 37*, 85-95.

102. Navalani, K. (1990). Manpower in university libraries in India: A study into level of its satisfaction with its status. *CLIS observer, 7*, 20-24.

103. Nazotta, B.C. (1985). A comparative study of job satisfaction of academic and public libraries in Nigeria. *African Journal of Academic Librarianship, 2*, 36-46.

104. Nazotta, B.C. (1985). Factors associated with job satisfaction of male and female librarians in Nigeria. *Library Information Science Research, 7*, 75-84.

105. New Standard Encyclopedia (1981). Chicago: Standard Educational, Vol.10.

106. Nisha, M. (1992). Women's status: An indicator of nation's progress. ***In*** Najma Heptulla (Ed.), *Reforms for women: Future options*. New Delhi: Oxford.

107. Nkereuwen, E.E. (1986). Issues in correlation between job performance and work behaviour among the staff in academic libraries. *African Journal of Academic Libraries, 4*, 10-17.

108. Nkereuwn, E.E. (1990). Issues on the relationship between job attitudes and work behaviour among the staff in academic libraries in Nigeria. *Information Services and Use, 12*, 253-261.

109. Oladokun, S.O. (1993). A survey of job satisfaction among library officers in Nigeria. *Library Review, 42*, 38-43.

110. Onohwakpor, J.E. (2003). A survey of staff relationship among senior and junior staff in Delta State University Library, ABRAKA. *International Library Movement, 25*, 97-106.

111. Palmer, C. and East, D. (1993). Job satisfaction among support staff in twelve ohio academic libraries. *College and Research Libraries, 54*, 43-57.

112. Panigraphy, R.L. and Nayak, S.S. (2011). Women entrepreneurship. New Delhi: Discovery Pub, 311.

113. Panneerselvam, R. (2007). *Research Methodology.* New Delhi: Prentice Hall.

114. Pascoe, C. (1996). Impact of an integrated information management system on the job characteristics, satisfaction and motivation of library staff. *Australian Library Review, 13*, 135-146.

115. Pestonjee, D.M. (1981). *Development of a psychometric measure of job satisfaction.* (Research Report).

116. Pestonjee, D.M. (1973). *Organizational structures and Job attitude.* Calcutta: Minerva Associates

117. Plate, K.H. and Stone, E.W. (1974). Factors affecting librarian's job satisfaction: A report of two studies. *Library Quarterly, 44*, 97-110.

118. Poffenberger, A.T. (1942). *Principles of applied psychology.* New York: Harper.

119. Pollard, G. (1995). Job satisfaction among : The influence of professionalism, perceptions of organizational structure and social attributes.

Journalism and Mass Communication Quarterly, 72, 682-697.

120. Prabhakar, V. K. (2001). *Research methodology and system analysis.* New Delhi: Anmol.

121. Pradhan, S. (2006). Women in library management. *Herald of Library Science, 45*, 63-66.

122. Prasad, H.N. (1994). Job anxieties and job satisfaction among professional library employees: A study. *Annals of Library Science and Documentation, 41*, 41-54.

123. Prasad, H.N. and Singh, S.N. (1990). Study into the effect of job anxiety on job satisfaction of professional library staff: A case study. *ILA Bulletin, 25*, 199-213.

124. Prida, B. (1992). *Status and job satisfaction of librarians in college and universities of Orissa. An evaluation in Indian context.* Ph.D. Thesis. Bhubansheswar: Utkal University.

125. Prins, H. (1991). Status, image and reputation of librarianship: Results of an empirical study. *Journal of Library and Information Science, 16*, 11-24.

126. Prytherch, R. (2000). *Harrod's librarian's glossary and reference book..* (9th . ed). England: Gower.

127. Rahman, Z. (2005). *Women and society.* Delhi: Kalpaz Publications.

128. Rajyalaxmi, D. (1999). Women in librarianship: Problems and prospects. ***In*** K Navalani and S. Trikha (Ed.), *Library and information services..* Jaipur: Rawat Publications.

129. Ramesh, L.S.R.C.V. and Raju, A.V.S.S. (2002). Lack of job satisfaction kills professionalism.

International Library Movement, 24, 126-131.

130. Rao, S.N. (1986). *Work adjustment and job satisfaction of teachers.* Delhi: Mittal.

131. Rayman, R. Goudy, F.M. (1980). Research and publication requirement in university libraries, *College and Research Libraries, 41*, 43-48.

132. Raza, M.M and Gupta, A (2000). Job satisfaction and job anxiety among library professional employees working in Delhi University Library System (DULS), *IASLIC Bulletin, 45*, 129-134.

133. Reddy, C.R. (1986). *Changing status of educated working women.* Delhi: B.R. Publishing Company.

134. Reddy, G.N. (1985). Role of women in economy and society. ***In*** *M.S. Mortan* (Ed.), *Women and child development: Some contemporary issues.* (pp. 4-12). Allahabad: Chugh Publications.

135. Ritchie, S. (1982). Women in library management. ***In*** Anthony Vaughn (Ed.), *Studies in library management.* v. 1. (pp.13-36). London: Clive Birgley :.

136. Rockman, I.F. (1984). Job satisfaction among faculty and librarian: A study of gender, autonomy and decision-making opportunity. *Journal of Library Administartion, 53*, 43-56.

137. Rohatagi, S. (1998). Women executives and social scenario. *Indian Management, 27*, 12-18.

138. Roy, Kumkum (2011). Women in early Indian societies. New Delhi: AJ software publishing,335.

139. Russell, N. (1984). *Job satisfaction of non-professional library staff.* Unpublished M.Phil. Thesis. CNAA: Leeds Polytecnic.

140. Sadeh, N. and Syacra, K. (1995). Back tracking techniques for the job shop scheduling constraint

satisfaction problem: *Artificial Intelligence, 76,* 455-480.

141. Sahaya, Amita and Kaistha, Sunita (2010). Women work and health: current concerns. New Delhi: The Women Press,280.
142. Samantaray, M. (1998). *Indian Women in librarianship.* New Delhi: National Book Organization.
143. Sangam, S.L. (1996). *Job satisfaction of librarians in Karnataka University library and its constituent colleges.* ***In*** Kumar, PSG and Vashishth, CP (Eds.). *Human relations in librarianship: Seminar papers of XLI All India Library Conference,* (pp. 53-66) *Vijaywada,* 7-10th Jan., Delhi: *ILA.*
144. Sanghi, S. (2001). A study of the motivational climate in relation to job satisfaction and organizational commitment. *Abhigyan, 18,* 19-25.
145. Satija, M.P. (2003). Academic status of librarians as perceived by sociologists. *ILA Bulletin, 39,* 5-10.
146. Scamell, R.W. (1980). A study of age and tenure as it pertains to job satisfaction. *Journal of Library Administration, 1,* 3-18.
147. Schneidar, M.S. (1991). Stress and Job satisfaction among employees in a public library system with a focus on public service. *Library and Information Science Research, 13,* 385-404.
148. Schumacher, E.F. (1980). *Good Work.* Abacus: London.
149. Sergean, R. (1976). *Librarianship and information work: Job characteristics and staffing needs.* London: British Library, Research and Development Department. (Report no. 5321 H.C.) V. *62,* 30.

150. Sharma J.S. (1977). Whither library profession. *Indian Librarianship, 31*, 168-173.

151. Sharma, J.N. (2007). *Research methodology: Discipline and its dimensions.* New Delhi: Deep and Deep.

152. Sharma, Sangeeta (2010). Women's liberation: the Arya samaj movement in India. Jaipur: Rawat, 318.

153. Shetty, Y. (1982). Management role in declining productivity. *California Management Review, 25*, 33-47.

154. Siggins, J.A. (1992). Job satisfaction and performance in a changing environment. *Library Trends, 42*, 299-315.

155. Simmons, N. (1980). Job satisfaction and styles of supervision among libraries in a London Borough. *Assistant Librarians, 73*, 132-134.

156. Singh, A. (2004). *Organizational Behaviour: Theory and Practice'*. New Delhi. Mohit.

157. Singh, J. and Kumar S. (2006). *Data collection and analysis*. Chennai, Indian Sociological Society.

158. Singh, M. (1975). *A study of job satisfaction of library professionals in relation to organizational climate and personal characteristics*. Ph.D. Thesis. Gwalior: Jiwaji University.

159. Singh, S.P. (2002). *Research methods in social sciences: A manual for design questionnaires*. New Delhi: Kanishka.

160. Sinha, J.B.P. (1981). Organisational dynamics ***In*** Udai Pareek (Ed.), *A survey of research in psychology* 1971-76, pt. 2. Bombay: Popular Parkashan.

161. Smith, P.C., Kendal, L.M. and Hulin, C.L. (1969). *The measurement of satisfaction in the work and retirement: A strategy for the study of attitudes.* Chicago: Rand McNally and Company.

162. Sommer, R. and Sommer, B.B. (1986). *A practical guide to behavioural research: Tools and techniques.* New York: Oxford University Press.

163. Sornam, S.A. and Sudha, S. (2003). Occupational role stress on women librarians: A study. *SRELS Journal of Information Management, 40*, 147-153.

164. Srivastava, A.K. (1983). Job satisfaction: Myth and reality. *Indian Journal of Labour Economics, 26*, 71-85.

165. Stamm, K. and Underwood, D. (1995). How pagination affects job satisfaction of editors. *Journalism and Mass Communication Quarterly, 7*, 851-862.

166. *Status of women in India*: A report (1975). New Delhi : Indian Council of Social Science Research.

167. Stead, B.A. and Scamell, R.W. (1981). A note on the contribution assertiveness training to job satisfaction of professional librarians. *Journal of Library Administration, 51*, 380-389.

168. Swarajalaxmi, C. (1992). *Women at work: Insights from Indian organisations.* New Delhi: Discovery.

169. Talwar, U. (1984). Why do women seek employment. ***In*** *Social profile of working women.* Jodhpur. Jain Brothers.

170. Tefko, S. (1981). *Consolidation of information. A handbook of evaluation, restructuring and repacking of scientific and technical information.* Paris: UNISIST (UNESCO).

171. Thapisa, A.P.N. (1991). The motivation syndrome:

job satisfaction through the pay nexus. *International Library Review, 23,* 141-158.

172. Thornton, J.C. (2001). African American female librarians: A study of job satisfaction. *Journal of Library Administration, 33,* 141-164.

173. Thornton, J.K. (2000). Job satisfaction of librarians of African descent employed in ARL academic libraries. *College and Research Libraries, 61,* 217-32.

174. Tull, D.S. and Albaum, G.S. (1973). *Survey research: A decisional approach.* New York: Intertext Books.

175. Ustun, A. (2002), Job satisfaction in information centres: A comparative study in Istanbul. *Library Progress, 22,* 1-12.

176. Vaughn, W.J. (1972). *Predictors correlates and consequences of job satisfaction in a university library.* Dissertation North Texas State University: Graduate School of Business Administration.

177. Vaughn, W.J. and Dunn, J.D. (1974). A study of job satisfaction in six university libraries. *College and Research Libraries, 35,* 163-177.

178. Verma, S. (1992). *Women's development: Policy and administration.* Jaipur : Aalekh Publishers.

179. Voelck, J. (1995). Job satisfaction among support staff in Michigan academic librarires. *College and Research Libraries, 56,* 157-70.

180. Vroom, V.H. (1964). *Work and motivation.* New York: John Wiley.

181. Wahba, S.P. (1975). Job satisfaction of librarians: A comparison between men and women. *College and Research Libraries, 36,* 45-51.

182. Wahba, S.P. (1975). Motivation, performance and

job satisfaction in libraries. *Library Journal, 71*, 270-278.

183. Wahba, S.P. (1978). Motivation, performance and job satisfaction in libraries. *Law Library Journal, 71*, 270-278.

184. Waters, D.H. (1988). New technology and job satisfaction in university libraries. *LASIE, 18*, 103-108.

185. Webster's *Third New International Dictionary of the English Language* (1981). V.2. Chicago: G and C Merriam.

186. Weiss, D.J. et al., (1967). *Manual for Minnesota Satisfaction Questionnaire.* Industrial Relations Centre. University of Minnesota: Minneapolis.

187. Whitlatch, J.B. (1991). Automation and job satisfaction among reference librarians. *Computers in Libraries, 11*, 32-34.

188. Williamson, J.M. (2005). An investigation of career and job satisfaction in relation to personality traits of information professionals. *Library Quarterly, 75*, 122-141.

189. Wood, F.E. (1975). Scientists in librarianship and information work: Survey of former information studies students of the postgraduate school of librarianship and information science, university of Scheffield, 1964-1973. *Journal of Librarianship, 7*, 32-48.

190. Woodruff, C.K. (1980). Data processing people – Are they satisfied with their job? *Information and Management, 3*, 219-225.

191. Yogi, M.M. (1967). *On the Bhagavad Gita: A new translation and commentary with Sanskrit text.* New Zealand: Penguin Books.

192. Zeffane, R. (1994). Computer usage and job satisfaction: An empirical exploration. *Information Management and Computer Security, 2*, 10-22.

193. Zimbardo, P.G. (1985). Psychology of life. ***In*** Nirmal Singh (Ed.), *Organizational behaviour.* (P. 263) Glenview, III. Scott Foresman.

Index

Aggrawal, C.M. 24,25
Association of Research Libraries ARL 52,58
Bengali Library Association 37
British Library Association 35
Centre for library and information management (CLAM) 46
Comparative analysis 187-188
Correlation 145-161
Correlational analysis 188-189
Demographics 66-70, 120-129, 171-176
Determinats of job satisfaction 104-108
Dewey, Melvil 36-37
Education and women 28
Family, 116-117
Gibran, Kahlil 42
Herzberg 59-60
Hoppock, F. 9,42
Information technology 71-76
Intercorrelation 145-161
Ingrid parent 13
International labour organization 31
International women decade 1985-96 6
International women year 1994-95, 6
Job and family 116-17
Job descriptive index 44,46
Job descriptive inventory 60
Job satisfaction 9,44,54,59, 70-76, 97-101, 104-108,120-29,138-76, 183
Library association annual report 1978-80, 39
Library and information science abstracts (LISA) 100
Library journal 35
Librarianship and women 32-33
Library profession 11,131-38, 178
Library professional 12
Life satisfaction 117-19
Logistic model 92-93
Ministry of Labor 31
Minnesota satisfaction questionnaire 45, 47-48, 51, 56, 67, 71
Motivation 59, 109-112
Off-the-job motivation factors 103-104, 186-87
Online public access catalogue (OPAC) 72

On the job factors 101-103, 183-186
Participative management 70-71
Pearson 145
Personal data 189-93
Pilot study 90
Productivity/ performance 112-13
Profession 10
Professional development 193-95
Professional status of women 29
Professionalism 11
Promotion 115-16
Ranganathan, S.R. 85
Regression 161-165
Rensis Likert 109
Research 77-79
Research and development 19
Research methodology 80-82
Sampling techniques 86-88
Satisfaction dissatisfaction employees inventory 89
Social status of women 25
Stress 64-66
University Grants Commission 39
Vivekananda, Swami 23
Women after independence 28
Women dominated profession 35
Women during pre-independence 27
Women in librarianship 29,35
Women librarians 12, 32-33, 54, 138-70
Women power 25
Women status 37-38
Yogi, M.M.1
Young India 25